THE PARTY BOOK

THE PARTY BOOK

A practical guide to giving parties

Helen O'Leary

COLUMBUS BOOKS

LONDON

© 1988 Helen O'Leary

First published in Great Britain in 1988 by
Columbus Books Limited
19-23 Ludgate Hill, London EC4M 7PD

British Library Cataloguing in Publication Data
O'Leary, Helen
    The party book: a practical guide to giving parties
        1. Entertainments: Parties – Manuals
        I. Title
        793.2

        ISBN 0-36287-411-4

Typeset by Facet Film Composing Limited,
Leigh-on-Sea, Essex

Printed and bound by The Guernsey Press, Guernsey, CI.

Contents

Introduction

Does the thought of giving a party make you panic? Parties are an essential part of the social scene – and that means giving them as well as going to other people's. They can be a daunting prospect. Where do you start? Can you afford to give the sort of party you have in mind? How will you find the time?

This book is designed to help. Whatever your lifestyle or the state of your bank balance, there is a party that's right for you. The good news is that the social scene is now more flexible than ever before: there is an infinite variety of ways to entertain. Extravagant formal parties are back in fashion; but you can choose from a whole range of other less spectacular but equally enjoyable possibilities: the traditional dinner party, informal brunch or afternoon tea, a barbecue or picnic for the summer months. Family occasions are always with us – weddings, christenings, Christmas – but these too can be as lavish or modest, formal or informal as you choose to make them.

Your first task is to decide which kind of party you want to give. It might be a white-tie-and-taffeta affair where guests dance all night among potted palms... or perhaps an elegant dinner, where course follows course in irresistible succession while the conversation sparkles... or an informal supper, where friends relax and gossip around the kitchen table. Your decision will be influenced by the occasion, your tastes and circle of friends, and of course your budget.

Whatever kind of party you choose, its success depends on three basic ingredients: good food, plenty to drink and a good mix of people. By far the most important of these is people. My guess is that no amount of vintage Dom Pérignon would have made a room full of Montagues and

Capulets fizz. But get a group of old friends together and they'll have a ball on supermarket wine, anywhere. However, that is not to say that good parties just happen. They need careful thought and scrupulous organization. So turn to the relevant chapter and start planning.

People like parties. An invitation adds zip and sparkle to their working day and gives their lives a touch of romance. Throwing a party may demand a great deal more time, effort and money than being a guest. It's worth it, though: the excitement of the preparations and the pleasure of seeing your friends enjoy themselves are hard to beat. This book should inspire you to go to the best party ever – your own.

CHAPTER 1

Parties for crowds

Whether you have a burning desire to make your next birthday an unforgettable occasion, or are saddled with a socially-minded partner determined to invite most of the firm home to celebrate, entertaining large numbers of people demands careful preparation. You don't need to be a millionaire or a member of the leisured classes, though: some of the best parties are given by the busiest of people on the leanest of means.

What you *must* do is decide, right from the start, how much time and money you are prepared to invest. Then start planning in detail.

For speedy action, equip yourself with a notebook and pen, turn off the phone and settle down somewhere quiet with a large drink. Take a few deep breaths and try to assume a positive frame of mind. Feeling efficient is halfway to being efficient.

Concentrate first on *why* you want a party. Evaluate your reasons. Next decide what sort of party you want – when and where. Think the party through: budget, venue, guests, food, drink, arrival and departure details, dress, etc. Write everything down before you forget. Work out a timetable, listing every job. Fix another meeting with yourself in a few days' time to check estimates against your budget (particularly important if you intend to sub-contract any of the work).

PREPARATIONS
Parties for crowds fall naturally within one of the following categories:
(1) stand and shout: drinks-only affairs from approximately 7 till 9 p.m.;
(2) stand for your supper: from about 8.30 to 9 p.m.

onwards with drinks all the time and a buffet or fork-supper;

(3) the grand occasion – with or without dinner – where the champagne never runs out and the band never stops playing: a night for you and your guests to remember for ever.

Be sure you know which type of party you are giving right from the start and stick to your decision. Attempting to feed 25 not-quite-sober stragglers from an almost empty larder is a recipe for disaster.

Setting the scene

Setting the party scene requires a little imagination. You may not have the perfect venue, but with some lateral thinking you can disguise its worst defects and make the most of its good features. Concentrate on the factors that will contribute to your guests' enjoyment and comfort, and you'll find that the party spirit will take care of itself.

If your party is to be held at home but you hate the idea of hordes of people stamping over your precious pale-green carpets, think again: does the party have to be in your day-to-day living quarters? For my daughter's fifteenth birthday, fearing for our sanity as well as the furniture, we declared the house out of bounds. Instead we transformed the garage into a Bedouin tent, floodlit the surrounding courtyard, borrowed a quantity of white wrought-iron tables and chairs complete with parasols and made a tape of the sea beating on the shore. *Voilà*: an exotic summer party full of Eastern promise.

Go for the uncluttered look. Push large items of furniture against the walls to leave a central area free for circulation. Store away (in the next flat, if you're pushed for space and have friendly neighbours) superfluous small tables, delicate chairs, fur mats, Persian carpets and anything remotely precious. Parties are no time to show off your collection of silver snuffboxes. Sadly, it could be the last you see of them.

Minimize wear and tear on your home by taking a few sensible precautions. Treat soft furniture with a stain-resistant aerosol spray. Some very fussy people cover french-polished furniture surfaces with clingwrap, but I wouldn't recommend this: it may be sensible but it looks awful. If the worst happens and spills or burns occur, mop up where necessary (keep soda water close at hand for squirting on spilt red wine) and *smile* even if it nearly kills you. Much can be done with a little help from professional cleaning agents in the morning.

Organize good subdued lighting. Buy a coloured light bulb or get a dimmer fitted to the light switch. More detailed information about lighting is on pages 42-3.

Remember that heating and ventilation matter. Make sure the rooms are warm *before* guests arrive. If it gets too hot you can always open a window later. Check and if necessary adjust your central-heating clock in advance. A sudden temperature drop around midnight sends guests scurrying home in seconds.

Be broad-minded about smoking. Even if *you* have just given up there's no need to expect others to do likewise. Provide matches and plenty of ashtrays: you can never have too many. In an emergency use small saucers, ramekins or, better still, scallop shells from the fish-monger – anything to stop scorch marks.

Good flowers are expensive, but they can transform a room. Go for one stunning arrangement which your guests will see on arrival. Small, fussy posies, dotted about on windowsills, get lost in the crowd and are just one more thing likely to be knocked over.

Have music, music, music all the time. But take care: the wrong kind of music can drive your guests to drink or yawning home to bed; on the other hand, good music – carefully chosen with your guests' tastes and ages in mind – can set a party off with a swing and keep it on a high note all night. The type of music and the cost involved depends on the event: simple background music is sufficient for drinks parties or small gatherings. If you have a piano, a single pianist playing nostalgic 'thirties and 'forties num-bers can be very effective. A good DIY party tape is cheaper, assuming your recording equipment is suitable. But for a grand occasion, large gathering or indeed almost any party at which you plan to have dancing, you need professionals. They alone have the equipment, the expertise and the extensive range of music required to make the party swing. See pages 43-4 for information on how to hire music and discos.

. Keep the food and the chat areas separate. If you live in a small flat use your bedroom for the food if there is nowhere else. Remove from sight obvious bedroom paraphernalia. Set up a trestle table over the bed and cover it with a pretty tablecloth or sheet. To avoid long queues, keep the food and the drink areas separate too. Set up a proper bar with everything you need to hand – in the hall, under the stairs or anywhere reasonably accessible. A bar backing on to a wall must be three feet (one metre) away from it.

Be kind to your guests' best clothes. A treasured coat bundled beneath 40 others or left to be trampled underfoot is enough to make the best guest weep. Beg or borrow coat-hangers and a rail from your local dry-cleaners or perhaps your place of work. If the weather is bad, find a suitable place, possibly the bathroom, for dripping umbrellas and drenched waterproofs, well away from furs and other finery.

Show you really care. See that there is plenty of loo paper *in the loo* (it's of no use in the store cupboard). Put a brush, comb, hairspray, safety pins, antiseptic cream, paracetamol and a box of tampons in the bathroom, plus a pile of fluffy, clean hand-towels. Keep a supply of spare cuff links and back collar studs, and make sure you can lay hands on sleeping bags for unexpected guests.

Parking space is almost always limited, especially in cities. Your closest friends will surely know the form, but other guests unfamiliar with the area may need to be warned. Where large numbers are concerned seek assistance from a motoring organization or try to make alternative arrangements, such as hiring a coach and setting up various collection points.

Wise party-giving parents are tolerant of young people who opt to stay the night after a party. Don't try to billet girls on one side of the corridor, boys on the other. Forget all about times past or 'when I was young' – for them you *are* 500 years old. Go to bed and sleep soundly: there's usually safety in numbers.

Your friends are among your most precious possessions.

Their comfort and enjoyment should be your watchwords when setting the party scene.

Guests and how to invite them

People make a party. But it takes skill to get the right mix. The only real answer is to be ruthless, however painful. Hence rule one: no bores, ever.

Of course, money, space and the type of party will dictate to a large extent the size of your guest list. But to make sure the conversation sparkles whatever the occasion, always include:

- your best friends – that goes without saying;
- a few people you're not so keen on – it may be only you who dislike them;
- several unattached people – you are not running a Darby and Joan Club;
- a couple of stimulating, clashing personalities: sparks add sparkle to a party;
- the neighbours – they may not come, but at least they've been warned and are less likely to complain about noise;
- a few 'beautiful people': ask them to come early – you want them to be *seen*;
- at least one good listener.

On the other hand, people to avoid asking are:

- chronic alcoholics;
- elderly friends and relations who hate crowds and who would prefer to see you in quieter circumstances for a long chat;
- your best friend's recent husband, boyfriend or partner.

Invariably when you plan a party your first guest list is longer than your drawing room, garden or marquee could ever accommodate. It is, of course, true that plenty of interesting people crammed into a small room is infinitely preferable to twenty stragglers in a large barn. However, few people enjoy playing involuntary sardines, so here's a guide to recommended space requirements:

13

- for a drinks party: approximately 8 sq feet (0.7 sq metres) per person;
- for a buffet supper: 10 to 12 sq feet (0.9 to 1 sq metre) per person;
- for a properly-seated party with dancing: 15 to 20 sq feet (1.3 to 1.9 sq metres) per person (more about this in a moment).

In general terms, aim to fill the available space comfortably, allowing for the fact that people may drop out at the last moment for unforeseeable reasons.

For a drinks party you can afford to over-invite to some extent because arrivals and departures are staggered and relatively few people will stay for the entire evening. A good drinks party should be a delightful stage in the evening for your guests. Some may come early on the way to a dinner or a dance; others may arrive late from the office, in dire need of refreshing both mind and body.

Buffet parties and fork suppers require a more controlled approach. For a start, you must provide some seating. A good basic rule is to allow chairs for about one-third of your guests and to increase the amount as the average age of your guests rises. It's worth mentioning too that men, in general, dislike trying to eat while standing up. Many will hunt for a table, even if it means eating in the kitchen.

When it comes to organizing a dance or large formal dinner a few calculations are essential. You need an area for guests to meet and mingle; seated place settings; and additional space for dancing. The total space requirement per guest is 20 sq feet (2 sq metres); unless you use the reception area for dancing later, in which case you can get away with only 15 sq feet (4.5 sq metres) per guest.

Ten people can sit comfortably at a round table of 5 feet diameter. Reduce the table by 6 inches (15 cm) – i.e. make the round 4 feet 6 inches (135 cm) across – and you lose two places: the smaller table will accommodate only eight guests.

In every case allow 1 feet 8 inches (50 cm) chair clearance, and at least a 3-foot (1-metre) gangway between each table.

The manner in which you invite your guests will depend on the type of party in question. For casual Sunday morning drinks, impromptu suppers and dinner parties, a telephone call is both quick and practical, although many people still prefer to scribble a postcard. For any formal party, however, it's worth taking the time and trouble to send out proper invitations.

A formal written invitation sets the tone of any party. It provides your guests with precise information about the event and acts as a useful reminder.

Some people enjoy sending elaborate, be-ribboned invitations, but thick white cards, elegantly styled, are still the most practical. They are not only clear, they're sturdy, and they're not as easy to mislay as invitations on ordinary paper.

Whatever style you choose, an invitation is meant principally to inform. All written invitations must therefore contain the following data:

- the venue: remember to state the full address; include a separate map or clear directions if you're inviting friends from afar or if your house is off the beaten track – not everyone is familiar with your local one-way system.
- the times: stipulate the start time and, if appropriate, the duration (e.g. 6.30-8 p.m. or 7.30 for 8 p.m.), and if you plan to serve food *say so*; an indication of the party programme is also helpful, e.g. supper 10.30 p.m., carriages 2.45 p.m.
- the date: check it twice – it is so easy to read what you *think* it says rather than what it actually says once it's neatly typed or printed.
- the type of party: be considerate – warn your guests if you plan to gamble the night away, or trudge the streets singing carols for charity, or go on a treasure hunt.
- dress: indicate what *you* intend to wear and resist the temptation to change your mind later. It's no fun for guests to arrive at a party wearing 'something comfortable and casual' only to find the host in white tie and the hostess in a tiara. Likewise, if you want your friends to dress up as nursery-rhyme characters or pop stars, say so and give them ample warning so that they have time to exercise their ingenuity.

Note 'White tie' invitations call for an evening dress

15

tail-coat and white waistcoat (for men), with a stiffly starched wing-collar shirt and white tie. Ladies normally wear long dresses on such occasions, which would of course be formal. 'Black tie' means dinner-jackets for men, with dress shirts, cummerbunds and bow-ties. Ladies may wear long or short dresses according to current fashion. An invitation for 'suits' requires the men to wear a formal dark business suit – navy or dark grey. Ladies' dress will again depend on fashion, and the time of day.

• the address to which guests should send their reply.

Mrs James Bloggs
At Home

....

RSVP
23 Middleton Street   *Drinks*
Pinner   *7–9 p.m.*
Middlesex
HA6 1JU

This type of invitation is worth keeping in stock if you entertain frequently. Simply fill in the relevant information (possibly only the date is needed) and write the guests' full name on the top left-hand corner of the card.

Invitations for more formal parties should be printed specially for the occasion. Guests' names should be hand-written at the top left hand of the card.

*Liz and James Stewart
request the pleasure of your company
at a party* to be held at
Sevenacres, Calne, Wiltshire
on Saturday 4th May 1987*

*RSVP
Sevenacres
Calne
Wiltshire*   *7.30 for 8 p.m.*
Please bring this invitation with you   *Black tie*

*the reason for it (e.g. 'on the occasion of James' 40th Birthday' or 'to celebrate their Silver Wedding') may be mentioned here.

In the past, important invitations were always embossed. Nowadays most people use the hot-printing process called thermography which achieves almost the same raised effect at a fraction of the cost.

Whichever print process you choose, remember, when it comes to ordering your invitations, that even exceptional printers are not mind-readers. They can only produce what they are asked to provide.

For problem-free printing, arrange and type out or neatly print the relevant information on a sheet of A4. Check it. Take your sheet of paper (together with a model invitation, if you have one) to the printer. Ask to see a sample card and specimen typeface. Make sure that the printer can supply envelopes to fit your chosen card.

Request an estimate and ask how long the job will take. Add a safety margin of at least two weeks. Insist on seeing a proof before the full quantity is printed, and ideally ask someone not immediately involved to read it over to you: it is amazing how easy it is for the organizer to miss an error at this stage.

Always order more invitations than you actually need.

The extra cost is negligible (it is the artwork and typesetting that cost money, not the multiple copies). Remember that far-flung friends and relations may not be able to come but would still like to receive an invitation. Wise party-givers also keep a supply of invitations in reserve. Just occasionally a guest Second Eleven must be fielded.

Reckon on about a ten per cent refusal rate, with more around Christmas or if you live in a highly sociable area. Good timing is all. Most busy people live a hectic yet planned life, so for any sort of special occasion it is essential to send out your invitations in good time, preferably eight weeks ahead.

No matter how busy you may be, the names of your guests *must* always be handwritten, in plain blue or black ink. Use full names to avoid confusion. Watch the spelling and check any titles or forms of address in *Burke's Peerage*.

Likewise, the correct reply to a formal invitation should be handwritten on private stationery. The correct form is as follows:

Applegate
Barrow
Berkshire

Jane Smythson thanks Mrs Thomas Moon for her kind invitation for 21 November which she accepts with much pleasure.

9 October 1987

Note that invitations always are written in the third person. The date is placed at the foot of the acceptance.

An example of a refusal, on the other hand:

Applegate
Barrow
Berkshire

Jane Smythson thanks Mrs Thomas Moon for her kind invitation for 21 November but regrets that she is unable to accept owing to a previous engagement.

9 October 1987

Counting the cost

If you want to stay sane and solvent, work to a budget. Obviously the type of party (drinks, small supper party, late-night party with dancing, etc.), the number of guests and to some extent the venue will dictate the sum involved: another good reason to make your original plan flexible.

Decide how much you can afford to spend right from the start. Few people have unlimited reserves of cash for entertaining, and it is plainly foolish to entertain beyond your budget.

In the first instance, calmly draw up an estimate of every single item likely to cost money. The budget checklist on pages 20-21 should help. Be realistic: under normal circumstances, two small fishes will not feed 500 hungry mortals. Bear in mind that *all* staff in the 'eighties work principally for money, not for the good of other people's health. Remember to include possible overtime and service charges when you estimate costs.

If the total estimated cost of your dream party seems at first sight wildly beyond your bank balance, scrap the idea instantly. *On no account weaken.* Forget all about grand designs, disco décor, marquees, fabulous flower displays and fireworks. Instead, go away for a weekend, fall in love, buy a new dress, read Chekhov. Do anything to clear your mind. Several weeks later make a fresh start on a more modest plan... afternoon tea?

If, on the other hand, you feel the estimated expenditure is only mildly adrift, consider your priorities and adjust the plan to suit your pocket.

Five easy ways to save money are:
- go for a less ambitious function: e.g. a drinks party rather than a buffet supper;
- invite fewer guests;
- cook the food yourself;
- beg flowers from kind friends with large gardens;
- forget about hired help: persuade a couple of friends to help you serve the drinks and resolve to do the washing-up yourself, next morning. For other ways to delegate see pages 31-2.

It is disastrous either to skimp on drink or to serve inferior food in the hope that people won't notice – they will.

Budget checklist
Here is a list of items which may need to be accounted for in any party budget, however modest or grand. Naturally not all the items are applicable to every kind of party, but it is easy to forget quite expensive aspects of a party, not least the dreaded VAT, in times of stress.

☐ Invitations (to include artwork and printing)
☐ Postage
☐ Hire of venue (hall, boat, hotel, marquee, etc.)
☐ Heating and lighting
☐ Hire of tables, chairs, etc.
☐ Hire of cutlery
☐ Hire of crockery
☐ Hire of glassware
☐ Hire of linen
☐ Removal of your own furniture
☐ Flowers and decorations
☐ Special effects/lighting
☐ Food
☐ Caterer's fee
☐ VAT on the caterer's bill
☐ Caterer's tips
☐ Drinks
☐ Ice
☐ Barman's/other staff's fee
☐ Hire of special bar equipment (shakers, ice buckets, etc.)
☐ VAT on bar staff
☐ Tips for bar staff
☐ Other helpers (cloaks, cleaners, washers-up, car-parking attendants, etc.)
☐ Possible overtime charge for above staff
☐ Refreshments and transport for staff
☐ Entertainment (cabaret, children's entertainers, fireworks, aerobatics team, marching bands etc.)
☐ Music (solo musician, big band, disco)
☐ Place cards
☐ Table presents
☐ Menus

☐ Seating plans
☐ Programmes
☐ Security
☐ Transport, including taxis
☐ Car parking
☐ Rubbish disposal
☐ Donation to St John's Ambulance or the Red Cross for
  first-aid cover
☐ Your new clothes
☐ Your hairdresser, manicurist, etc.

Always ask for written estimates for any work contracted out. Arrange for two or three firms to submit quotations. That way you can gain a clear idea of the market and compare prices. Watch out for hidden extras: staff overtime, VAT and, if you live outside the town from which you are hiring services, a mileage addition.

FOOD AND DRINK

If you hated your last party, the chances are that the food was the culprit. It took too long to prepare. You were exhausted before the party began, or you had to be in the kitchen half the evening. In future, forget about complicated cookery and resolve to have more fun. Resist the temptation to copy TV chefs, who are always able to produce with a flourish the dish they happened to have 'prepared earlier', or to follow advice from cookery writers who forget that you might want to *talk* to your guests. Instead, aim for simple, welcoming food. Organize some help in the kitchen or, if you are the cook, choose food with which you are familiar and which can be prepared for the most part in advance, allowing you to join in and enjoy the party too.

Catering for crowds can be subdivided into three main categories:

• drinks and cocktail party nibbles;
• buffet and fork-supper fare;
• formal luncheon or dinner.

Drinks and cocktail party nibbles

The provision of original, bite-sized, light, nourishing and reasonably non-fattening fare is an essential ingredient for a successful drinks party. Good food keeps the conversation flowing and the guests upright. Handing round a dish of delicious goodies also provides shy newcomers with an opportunity to mix. Your selection need not be vast but the food offered must be fresh, appetizing and easy to eat – and preferably of the non-drip variety. For a two- to two-and-a-half-hour party, allow six to ten nibbles per person, of which half should be reasonably substantial (to act as blotting paper).

The fact is, however, that cocktail party food is *very* labour-intensive, and you must be prepared to plan and cook ahead. Here are a few simple ideas to add to your list of familiar favourites:

baked honey sausages and mild mustard
apricot halves stuffed with cream cheese
warm stuffed mushroom caps
cream cheese balls rolled in chopped chives
prawn and ginger cream dip
smoked salmon or prawn pâté on cucumber rounds
bacon-wrapped prunes or, better still, apricots
mange-tout (blanched) wrapped round prawns
stuffed quails' eggs in a basket lined with frisée or alfalfa
    (add a hard-boiled hen's egg with the yolk scooped out to
    form a cup half-filled with celery salt)
water chestnuts wrapped in streaky bacon and grilled till
    crisp
interesting crudités: blanched french beans, mange-tout,
    tiny broccoli sprigs, strawberries or miniature corn on
    the cob.

Presentation is all-important for cocktail party food. That is not to suggest you fiddle about making radish roses – far from it. The art of serving cocktail party food lies not so much in elaborate garnish, but more in common sense and an eye for detail.

Always consider the colour and texture of the food you wish to present. Before the party, arrange the food on several small dishes. Offer one or two at a time (depending on the number of guests). Switch empty or half-filled plates with replacements from the kitchen. Being urged to choose food from a picked-over plate is awful: the smoked salmon has always long gone. Big platters are not just unwieldy to manoeuvre, they quickly look a mess.

Arrange canapés of the same kind (two or three at the most) in rows, preferably on individual dishes. Scattered mixtures look untidy. Cocktail food is best presented on simple white china or in shallow wicker baskets lined with napkins. You may prefer to use silver salvers (remember to line them against acid foods), stainless steel dishes, foil-covered trays, or even biscuit tin lids. Avoid using containers that are either too heavy or too precious, and remember that small bunches of fresh herbs, flowers or watercress help to make cocktail food look interesting.

There is nothing like an electric hotplate or tray for keeping cocktail food hot without letting it spoil. Beg or borrow one for late autumn or winter parties. A microwave oven can be useful too.

If, on the other hand, you really cannot face the prospect of cutting canapés for hours, never mind clearing up the mess involved, the answer is to call in the caterers. Good caterers, be they representatives from a large company or a local freelance cook, will supply a selection of canapés chosen by you in advance from their list. Charges for cocktail party food are usually made on a *per capita* basis. When you first see the estimate, don't faint. Remember, it's not just the food you are paying for, but also the labour.

Buffet and fork-supper fare
Everlasting coronation chicken and nondescript pâté, alone or palely loitering among the withered lettuce leaves, cast an air of gloom over any buffet party. Like running out of drink, it is guaranteed to drive your best friends home or to the nearest pub in a deep depression.

The trouble lies not so much in the choice of ingredients but in over-reliance on the food processor, an invaluable piece of kitchen equipment which can sometimes, unfortunately, lead to bland and predictable dishes. Buffet food is likely to taste refreshingly different without it.

What you need for a buffet supper is simple, tasty, recognizable food, which is easy to prepare, serve and eat.

Away with the mint-jellied lamb chops, jumbo prawns in their shells, sawdust pâté and anything smothered with chaud-froid sauce or aspic.

Here's my blueprint for the perfect buffet party menu: one giant 'dish of the day' (in winter a heart-warming goulash or juicy boeuf bourguignon; in summer chicken à la king or blanquette de veau) plus a platter of very thinly sliced cold meats; plenty of interesting salads; French bread; followed by fresh fruit in season, or good home-made chocolate gâteau, or a couple of impressive open French fruit tarts, plus cheese.

Arrange the buffet table so that you have free access to the kitchen. For any party with over a dozen people, allow more than one point of service if possible. Indicate the sections with piles of plates and sets of silver and napkins and show people where to help themselves. At buffet parties, guests are frequently reluctant starters, as they hate to appear too keen to get at the food. Polite queues linger behind the first point of service, unwilling to move ahead to the next. A good hostess tactfully helps guests move on by indicating the next section, saying something like, 'There are more plates and forks further along – do come and help yourselves.'

Finally, when you plan a buffet menu please remember that forks do *not* cut. Even if you do provide knives, few of your guests will be blessed with three hands. However, there are now some practical plastic gadgets on the market which clip on to plates to hold a glass: not exactly gracious living, but practical and worth a try. Beware: the type currently available fits only goblet glasses.

Formal luncheon or dinner
Dinner parties – elegant meals for eight, ten or twelve – are dealt with in Chapter 3. Here let's consider a formal seated meal for a larger number of guests.

If you're a good cook, the chances are that you may at some time consider catering for this type of party yourself. My advice is: *don't*. Providing a formal, sit-down meal for more than ten people, unaided, is an almost impossible task. Never mind the practical details (clearing plates, refilling glasses, carving the meat, passing vegetables – all at the same time), the sight of a harassed hostess makes even the most relaxed guest feel guilty and uncomfortable. So if funds are low or outside help unobtainable, be firm with yourself, recognize your limitations and stick to the much easier self-service, buffet-style meal.

If you can afford outside help and want to entertain a large group of friends, bear in mind that the choice of menu depends not just upon your personal taste and budget. The meal offered should be balanced, nourishing and seasonal. A wise choice will also consider the average age of your guests: rarely do the very young or the very old enjoy highly spiced or unfamiliar exotic foods. Colour is another important factor: while the food should be aesthetically pleasing, psychedelic colour schemes are likely to deaden the palate of all but the colour-blind.

Even with the aid of a caterer, simplicity is the key to success when it comes to feeding large numbers. Choose uncomplicated dishes with a wide appeal. For smooth operation in the kitchen the tried-and-tested formula of cold starter, hot main course and cold pudding still works best. For the most part it pays to be guided by your chosen caterer, but there are a few points which should always be borne in mind.

Avoid repetition: red soup followed by red stew, followed by red fruit salad; garlic bread, garlic prawns, garlic lamb, etc. Similarly, pastry should not be served at more than one course.

A surfeit of cream and eggs could give your guests dyspepsia. The inclusion of one richly-sauced dish is sufficient for any menu.

How much for how many?
More people does not necessarily mean proportionately more food. Strange as it may seem, the greater the number of people there are at a party, the less food each person will eat. Simply multiplying a single portion by the number of guests is clearly not the answer when catering for large numbers, unless you and the cat wish to live on leftovers for the rest of the week. Only you know the likely appetites of your friends. Caterers, on the other hand, usually work to a portion-controlled system.

Here is a rough guide to help you estimate the basics:

	Single serving	24 servings
Pâté	3-4 oz (75-100 g)	5-6 lb (2-2.5 kg)
Fish	4-5 oz (100-150 g)	5-6 lb (2-2.5 kg)
Meat with bone	5-6 oz (150-175 g)	7-9 lb (3-4 kg)
Meat without bone	4-5 oz (100-150 g)	6-7 lb (2.5-3 kg)
Rice	2 oz (50 g)	3 lb (1.8 kg)
Pasta	2 oz (50 g)	2-3 lb (900 g-1.5 kg)
Vegetables	4 oz (100 g)	6 lb (2.5 kg)
Lettuce	⅙	4-5
Tomatoes	1-2	3 lb (1.5 kg)
Cucumber	1 inch (2 cm)	2
Mayonnaise	1-2 fl oz (30-60 ml)	2 pints (1 litre)
French dressing	1 fl oz (30 ml)	½-2 pints (300 ml-1 litre)
Cheese	2-3 oz (50-75 g)	3-4½ lb (1.2-1.8 kg)
Biscuits	2-3	50-75
Coffee		⅓ pint (200 ml): 4 oz (100 g) coffee; 6 pints (3 litres) water; 2 pints (1 litre) cream (to be served separately)

A 10-inch (25-cm) gâteau will cut into 16-20 slices, depending how rich and how deep it is.

A 2-litre tub of ice cream provides 25-30 scoops.

For fresh-fruit salad allow 1 large piece of fruit per person.

1 French stick generally serves six and requires 4 oz (100 g) butter.

Delicious party drinks

Champagne is undoubtedly the perfect party wine, although, sadly, the genuine article is often too expensive for most of us to consider when entertaining large numbers. But you can still have bubbles on a budget.

There are three types of fizz:

(1) real champagne: this may be vintage (very expensive indeed) or non-vintage, which costs rather less. Use according to your budget for special occasions or when you're feeling rich and do not plan to serve mixed drinks;
(2) *méthode champenoise*: sparkling white wine made in precisely the same way as champagne but not from the clearly defined Champagne region of France; this type of wine costs less than champagne but more than the carbonated varieties; use for mixed drinks such as Kir Royale;
(3) sparkling wine: an inexpensive carbonated wine (in other words, the bubbles have been put into an ordinary still wine): while light on both purse and alcohol content, the carbonation may leave you with splitting headache and an amazing thirst next morning, so it is not really to be recommended.

Ways to offer bubbles on a budget:

• Buck's Fizz: half champagne, half orange juice: this immediately halves overall bottle consumption;
• old-fashioned champagne cocktails, with a sugar lump in the base of the glass: this kind of mixture is so strong that few will be in a position to drink more than two or three glasses;
• mixed drinks: Bellini (champagne and peach juice), Kir Royale (champagne and cassis) or the currently fashionable champagne and raspberry liqueur (add a tiny dash of Grand Marnier for extra zip as they do in Paris); the addition of fruit juice overpowers the fine flavour of the wine in every case; Dom Pérignon would be wasted, so use a respectable *méthode champenoise* instead. Buy the type labelled 'brut'.

For a cocktail party, unless you can afford to employ experienced professional staff, the best solution is to have one or two simple mixtures, appropriate to the time of the year and the temperature, which can be served from glass jugs. Any attempt to shake, stir and serve individual drinks unaided is a recipe for disaster. If you are giving a party single-handed, one answer is to persuade a couple of good friends to help keep the jugs topped up and the glasses filled.

Cocktail mixtures vary in spirit content and recipes number a legion. However much fun it may be to sip alarming alcoholic concoctions, bedecked with paper parasols and plastic swizzle-sticks, when on holiday in the sun, they may not be suitable for the weather and ambiance of your home territory. If you must have a complicated mixed cocktail, invest in one of the many excellent books currently available on the subject, but forget the paper accessories.

Other stylish drinks useful for theme drinks parties include:

- Bloody Mary: good for a red theme party (very filling);
- Black Velvet: but beware, not everyone feels Guinness is good for them.
- Glühwein: good for ski-mad friends, Christmas, Guy Fawkes' Night or carol-singing parties.
- Pimm's: delicious on a hot day; even better for your waistline if you use low-calorie lemonade.
- Punch: a soggy fruit salad full of flowers, lemonade and a lot of other unidentified floating objects will just *not* do. Indeed, punch of any sort will *never* do for teenagers: they're convinced that it's an attempt to ration their alcohol intake. For any other age group a good punch can look and taste wonderful. Use a proper punch bowl (you can hire one from a catering hire company) or a pretty antique china bowl (not a kitchen mixing bowl) and decorate just before serving with crisp, freshly-sliced fruit.

Always either prepare mixed drinks yourself or employ professional bar staff. Clever-Cloggs from next door, eager to lend a hand, may think it amusing to add more alcohol than the recipe stipulates. He may not know that over-intoxicating drinks have no style at all.

Opening sparkling wine is an art many people find difficult to master, but exploding corks can be danger-ous and foaming wine which spills everywhere is a terrible waste, so it's worth knowing how to avoid both.

Make sure the bottle is well chilled, and do not shake or move it violently. Remove the foil surrounding the wire cage and untwist the wires, keeping your free hand over the cork for safety. (Corks have been known to fly out at this stage.) Hold the bottle at a 45-degree angle to your body, always away from your face. Hold the cork firmly with your right hand and twist the bottle round the other way with your left, gently easing it away from the cork.

When you choose wine for a buffet supper or formal seated dinner, do not assume that the most expensive wine is necessarily the best. Some wines are too young and need to be kept a year or two; some have been kept too long; some may have been handled carelessly. A good wine merchant will be aware of these problems and well qualified to help you choose something appropriate to your party and your pocket. Discuss the party and the menu with him or her. Talk about money: be realistic and say how much you are prepared to spend. Be open-minded: non-classic wines (i.e. those not from Burgundy or Bordeaux, but produced in the lesser-known wine regions of France, as well as America and Australia) can be very good buys. For special dinner parties, a knowledge of vintages (from a vintage chart) can help you make a suitable selection for the meal.

At a party, plenty of everyday, drinkable wine is infinitely preferable to rationed thimblefuls of fine wine or expensive malt whisky.

How much wine you need will depend upon the type and duration of your planned party. Professional caterers always make wine go much further than amateurs. One reason is that they never quite fill a glass. However, most wine merchants (not supermarkets) deal on a sale-or-return basis (full sealed bottles only). Over-estimation can therefore do no harm, whereas running out of drink is a cardinal sin. Don't panic, though, if drinking seems fairly brisk in the early stages of a party – almost all, bar the serious drinkers, will slow down eventually.

For drinks parties where mixed drinks are being served, allow half to two-thirds of a bottle per head. For dinner parties, reckon on a bottle per head. Match the wine to the food: as a general rule, serve white with the starter or fish and red with the meat course.

Long, special-occasion evening parties with dancing are more difficult. Here you need to cater for an aperitif, wine to go with the meal, plus perhaps port or brandy after dinner, as well as possible drinks later.

The following information may help you steer a straight course through the drinks maze:

- an average wine glass holds 5 fl oz (142 ml);
- a typical bottle of wine will fill 6 glasses to a reasonable level;
- a litre bottle of wine will fill 8-10 glasses;
- a magnum of champagne contains 145 cl and fills 12-14 flutes;
- public houses squeeze 32 single measures from a 75-cl bottle of spirits.

Finally, when you order your party drinks, do remember that some people simply dislike alcohol, while others want only a very little. They are not being tiresome or priggish so please do not punish them with a dreary jug of cheap orange squash. Spare them some of your time and provide bottled mineral water, low-calorie Coke and if possible some interesting, freshly-pressed fruit juice. Drivers, Muslims, dieters and lots of normal, interesting people will appreciate this. If you intend to have dancing at the party it is also a good idea to organize a soft-drinks bar close to the dancing area, where your guests are likely to be hot and thirsty. Caribbean fruit juices, now available at many good supermarkets, are invaluable for enlivening the soft drinks repertoire.

HELPING HANDS

At a small party the hostess is often the cook, while the host acts as barman. However, attempting this kind of double-act for large numbers is not only daft, it's counter-productive – neither you nor your guests will enjoy the proceedings. The golden rule for entertaining more than ten people is to *get some help*.

A little assistance, not necessarily professional hired

help, can ease the strain and raise your morale. In fact, most experienced party-givers exercise the art of delegation to a high degree, so why not follow their lead? The secret lies in doing what you can do well and entrusting to others those tasks which you cannot undertake with confidence. For example: sons, husbands, men friends or friends' brothers can be roped in to help set the party scene, carry furniture, fix the lights and put up decorations. Hopeless but well-off cooks might consider hiring a professional caterer; the not-so-rich rest of us, hopeless or otherwise, have to cope. Nevertheless there are other ways to make entertaining less daunting. Most require you to spend some money – but not *much* money. Charm, ingenuity and just a little money will get you everywhere.

Seek out a good freelance cook and get her to make the puddings (or the starter, or the main course: whatever gives you the biggest headache). Check out the cost in advance. Bribe a culinary-oriented friend to bring the salads, or starter, or something. At times other than Christmas and Easter, when the crowds are horrific, go to a good food store and buy some ready-prepared food. It's expensive, but think of the time you'll save. Smile as you serve the prawn cocktail or the trout pâté: few will recognize the source.

Selected bachelors, wine buffs and sometimes young nephews (mine, aged eleven and thirteen, love to feel grown-up) enjoy pouring straightforward wine and topping up glasses. Arrange for a couple of teenagers (not necessarily girls – boys are often more willing) to come in and help on the day. You'll have to pay them something, but not nearly as much as professional staff.

Invite a keen flower-arranging friend who has a big garden and ask her to help you do the flowers. With a bit of luck she'll offer to take over and leave you free to get on with other things. Have a little present tucked away to give her later. On no account adopt the above tactics with friends who 'do flowers' professionally. It's just not fair. The same goes for professional cooks, cookery writers, bar staff, disco operators and anyone who relies on the paid party scene for his or her daily bread.

Never wash up, clean the kitchen, wash the floor or

vacuum the sitting room late at night after a party. Instead, put the cat out and *go to bed*. Stay with a friend if you can't face the mess in the morning. Get your usual cleaner, or the aforesaid teenage helpers, or a team of professional cleaners (see *Yellow Pages*) to come and clear up while you're at work next day. Expect to pay extra for this service.

The professionals
There are three things to remember when engaging professional caterers: be choosy about whom you employ, be direct about what you want, and be invisible on the day.

Choosing a caterer takes time and perseverance. As a general rule it is best to find outside help by word of mouth, and even better to have seen a company in action. Failing that, extensive field research is your only hope of success. At the back of this book is a short list of well-known caterers, party planners, etc. For a more comprehensive selection look in upmarket/society magazines.

Whether you use a caterer who is completely unknown to you or a tried-and-tested establishment, the procedure is the same. First, ring up and approach at least three suitable establishments. Ask for general details, price lists, menus, etc. Most are happy to supply the relevant information together with brochures and lists on request.

Next, arrange a meeting with a representative from each contractor with a view to obtaining a written quotation. Don't be put down by supercilious young men or women. It's *your* money they are proposing to spend. Likewise do not be impressed by lofty 'Leave it all to us, little lady' autocrats. Both types are likely to leave you with a giant inferiority complex.

Remember, it is *your* party, so conduct the meeting on your terms, in your own home if possible. If not, choose a venue where you feel at ease. Be businesslike. Draw up a list of items for discussion beforehand and be quite clear in your own mind about your priorities.

At the meeting, begin with your budget. Once that is firmly established you can both begin to plan the practical details. Discuss the menu, wines, service charge, tips, etc. Ask to see samples of the caterer's china and linen, together with photographs of table decorations and food. In addition allow the following thoughts to filter through your mind:

- Do you like the person?
- Does he or she understand what you are saying?
- Has he or she the skill and resources to interpret your wishes correctly?
- Are his or her standards similar to yours?
- What has not been said?

Once you receive the written estimates, take time to check them through thoroughly. Agree each item with the notes you made at the meeting. Make sure nothing has been left out; if it has, organize any necessary changes. When you consider the cost, remember that the cheapest estimate may not necessarily be the best. Look for hidden extras, such as mileage. Watch out for VAT, service charges, cover charges, overtime, staff transport and 101 possible extras, all of which could make a tremendous difference to the final account.

Your choice made, some catering establishments demand a deposit. Pay it with grace: a good caterer will serve you well and can become a life-long friend – likewise a good florist, wine merchant or band leader.

Big spenders with no time and plenty of cash to flash call in the party people (list on page 115), the entrepreneurs who take care of all problems on the party front. Some are excellent; others can prove disappointing, to say the least. Knowing which is which is the problem. As with most things, a good personal recommendation is worth more than any glossy brochure. On the other hand, remember that personalities matter when giving a party. You may detest on sight the young man your friend found so helpful.

If you engage a firm of party planners to organize the entire event, *insist* that an itemized costing is included with their estimate. That way you will retain overall control and be able to sleep soundly.

THEME PARTIES
A theme party can be a great success or a ghastly flop.

Planning and wearing fancy dress presents either an opportunity for happy anticipation or makes the heart sink, depending on your nature.

But whether you enjoy dressing up or not, the decision to hold a theme party should in no circumstances be undertaken lightly. A theme party involves a deal of hard work and it's up to the host or hostess to make most of the effort. Be warned, it's the effort of thinking that takes most time.

In the first instance if you plan a theme party, you must realize that it's futile to expect half a dozen people attired in ill-assorted fancy dress to create an authentic Jane Austen evening or a spectacular Space-Age rave-up. Your guests should merely *complete* the theme, dressing up, performing or playing games as requested.

Your job is to plan the celebration to reflect your chosen theme throughout the evening. Clearly this does not mean simply scribbling 'pink party' on the invitation while you slop cochineal into the sorbet. It means making time to design the decorations, search out the right props, organize the entertainment, sort out the music, select a suitable menu and order appropriate drinks – in addition to coping in the kitchen and being the perfect hostess.

If your budget is big enough, one of the many 'party people' (see the list on page 115) will willingly undertake the complete task for you for a substantial fee. This will leave you free to enjoy your theme party and worry about the bill the next morning.

For the not-so-rich who would like to throw a theme party, here are a few fresh ideas you might like to try. Just remember, whatever theme you choose, the object of the exercise is to get *everyone* to participate and join in the fun: guests, waiters, barmen – the lot.

Historical treasure hunt Mixed-age teams (previously advised to wear warm coats and wellies, if appropriate) compete to search out clues. Somehow these events tend to happen more often in winter, and hunters who have spent an afternoon in the crisp winter air will much appreciate the comforting support of steaming hot mulled wine. Afterwards, everyone re-assembles back at HQ for a huge farmhouse tea, ideally in front of a roaring fire. This party, particularly suitable for Boxing Day, when you are likely to have a suitable mix of ages ready assembled, is certainly inexpensive, but its success depends on careful organization. The clues must be well constructed and so cleverly concealed that teams will have to use considerable ingenuity to win the 'treasure'. The hostess must not only provide good grog and a splendid spread for tea: she has to spend weeks before the party poring over local history books researching the clues, and even longer encouraging local publicans, garage proprietors and farmers to help by pointing the treasure-hunters in the right direction.

Dodgems   This is a good way to make the night explode to the sound of ricocheting guests. Bumper cars bring out the anarchist in us all – and will send your friends home bruised but exhilarated (see page 117 for hire advice).

Edwardian picnic   Men in top hats and frock coats and bustled ladies in silk and muslin travel to a pre-selected picnic spot equipped with a traditional English spread: quails' eggs, salmon with mayonnaise, a huge ham, cold game pies, salads, home-baked breads, all carved and served by impeccably dressed chefs and waiters. Provide small tables and chairs so that guests can eat in comfort beneath shady trees. A small group of musicians playing chamber music or favourite Edwardian songs will complete the picture; failing live entertainers, old 78s and a wind-up gramophone might fit the bill.

Victorian musical evening   Hold this at Christmas-time and ask the guests to come as a character from a Victorian novel: Sherlock Holmes, Little Nell, Heathcliffe, Becky Sharp, Scrooge, Uncle Tom, Huckleberry Finn . . . Decorate your rooms with plenty of holly and mistletoe and engage a professional trio or quartet to play a programme of classical music. Restrict the playing time to 45 minutes each half. Arrange chairs in rows for the audience.

Greet guests with a glass of champagne and during the interval offer a Victorian supper. For an authentic look pile the buffet table with elaborate silver and glassware as well as the extravagant food. Offer cold consommé, lobster mayonnaise, cold duck, tongue and ham jelly, chicken cutlets, fruits piled into high towers, and French pastries.

Pit-stop party   This is best held outside the home. Decorate the barn or garage to resemble a racing garage with tyres, cardboard cut-out petrol pumps, racing-car posters, and drivers' portraits. Have the waiters dress as mechanics in jeans and T-shirts – but no grease. You need an authentic garage background of non-stop pop; and make the food 'fast' – chicken and chips, salad, followed by fruit and cheese. Guests wear casual gear.

Sukiyaki and sake party   Limit numbers for this Japanese feast. Late spring is the best time to entertain this way, when you can use masses of cherry blossom to decorate your rooms. Ask guests to wear Japanese kimonos. Greet them in the Japanese way, with hands together and a deep bow. Serve the meal on a low table about a foot (30 cm) high and ask guests to sit on the floor. Before the meal begins offer your guests hot rolled towels. Serve sukiyaki (thinly sliced sheets of topside or rump steak, beancurd, mushrooms, onions and other chopped vegetables cooked in a shallow pan with a seasoning sauce of soy sauce, *sake*, *mirin*, *dashi* and caster sugar at the table). Each person is provided with a bowl and chopsticks. While the meat is cooking each guest breaks an egg into his bowl and beats it with his chopsticks. Pieces of meat and vegetables are then taken from the pan and dipped in the egg before being eaten.

To drink, offer green tea or warm *sake*. The latter should be served in small china flasks and poured into tiny Chinese cups. To warm the *sake* place the bottle in a container of hot water. If you heat it in a pan the alcohol will be lost.

Play Japanese music, perhaps interspersed with songs from *The Mikado*.

Caribbean evening   Choose a summer evening and ask guests to wear Caribbean-style clothes: brightly coloured cottons, straw hats and beach sandals. Set the scene with plastic palm trees (you can hire these from theatrical props agencies). Have a tape playing of the sea beating on the shore in the background and reggae or steel band music on disc or tape. For the meal offer spicy Creole food: sweetcorn bread, salt codfish fritters, or pepper and avocado salad, followed by shrimp or beef creole, stuffed bananas, fresh mangoes. To drink, serve a rum punch before the meal and a robust red wine with the food.

'**Thirties soirée**   Plenty of potted palms, a pianist (or trio) and ballroom dancing make this theme. A cabaret singer is also a good idea. Ask your guests to dress Fred and Ginger-style and serve cocktails when they arrive. Make the event a dinner dance, that is to say, dancing takes place *between* courses as well as later. Keep the food simple but interesting: avocado and prawns, one hot dish (lamb cutlets, for example), then a fruit salad. Offer wine with the meal and plenty of mineral water to refresh the dancers.

Arabian feast   The good thing about this theme is that creating the interior of a Bedouin tent is not too difficult. But you will need yards and yards of thin material or a quantity of coloured sheets to billow from the ceiling. Cover low tables or old-fashioned junior-school benches or small forms with Persian rugs and scatter large cushions for your guests to lounge upon rather than using conventional seating. (Store all chairs out of sight.) Ask guests to wear Arabian gear, that is, long flowing robes (djellabas) and turbans for the men; long black cloaks, later removed to reveal bright silk dresses or evening trousers and tops, for the women. For the entertainment aim to provide a scene from the *Arabian Nights,* have a couple of jugglers, a snake charmer and belly dancer wander among the guests. Make the music Arabic. You can buy tapes from any good multi-cultural record shop.

Drink mint tea and fresh orange juice (perhaps adding vodka to the latter, though it's strictly non-authentic, to give the party a sparkle). For the meal offer *cous-cous* (a type of spiced lamb stew on a mound of semolina) or *harira* (a spicy fish soup) and for dessert a heavenly, sticky honey-and-almond confection, *baklava* (buy these from an ethnic grocer's). Authenticity could be further achieved by not providing cutlery – but you would probably be wiser not to go this far!

Indian Raj party   Serve a selection of curries and a vast quantity of mango chutney, side dishes, poppadoms and chapatis, lots of lime juice and cold beer or lager. (Wine is totally overpowered by curry.) However, make sure you also have a dish of plain cold meats or a simple roast chicken to offer guests who dislike spicy food. For clothes and scene-setting, think back to your favourite 'last days of the Raj' film or TV series (*A Passage to India, The Jewel in the Crown*) and take your inspiration from there. The appropriate theme music could help create the right mood; or you might like to play some authentic Indian sitar music.

Other ideas to turn over in your mind include the ever-popular 'pink' party (for pink food choose prawns, trout, salmon and offer pink champagne to drink . . . or for less money kir – white wine and cassis). For Bonfire Night or Hallowe'en serve up baked potatoes, sausages, pumpkin masks and apples for bobbing. For a St Andrew's Night party you need haggis, of course, with Scottish dancing and as much tartan as your guests can muster. An old-time music hall party with plenty of pearly kings and queens, Burlington Berties and Marie Lloyds is another promising theme, for which good costumes can be hired from theatrical agents.

CHAPTER 2

The dance of your dreams

This chapter is about putting on the glitz. If you want an evening where everything – from the table settings to the flowers and fireworks – matches perfectly, read on. And if it really is a once-in-a-lifetime, no-expense-spared occasion when everything must be absolutely right, my advice is to start planning at least a year ahead.

Entertaining several hundred people in a formal setting is a complicated business. Timing and co-operation are all-important. Make a start with the information given earlier on party planning: invitations, guest lists, engaging caterers and other staff, etc. All are applicable to the gala occasion. Your respective lists will be longer and take that much more time to compile, but that's all. In addition, there are quite a few other items which require close attention, together with one or two pitfalls worth avoiding.

VENUE
Entertaining a large number of people requires consider-able space, not only for the party itself, but also for the preparation of food and drink, for cloakrooms, coat rooms, sitting-out areas, parking, flower-arranging and decora-tion, etc.

One answer is to plan your party away from home (see below for suggestions). A much better idea, however, is to use bold decoration to transform your barn or garage, or better still hire a tent. Fear not. If the words 'marquee' or 'tent' conjure up visions of a grubby, off-white canvas tent on the edge of a cricket pitch, you're wrong. Marquees in the 'eighties are more like exotic, portable palaces.

Most contractors agree that no site is too difficult. You don't need a flat garden or a perfectly square house. Excellent marquees can be placed on sloping lawns, attached to oddly-shaped barns, erected over narrow back gardens or even on the roofs of high-rise buildings.

A good contractor (see pages 114-15) should be able to offer linings in almost any colour. Swathed silk linings look especially good if you add crystal chandeliers. Floors too are a matter of choice, and range from simple coconut matting to wall-to-wall Wilton. For a very special occasion, interiors can be made to look like a home with fireplaces, doors and French windows. The sprung dance floor can be sunken, or underlit, or even suspended over a swimming pool. You can even have a full-scale cloakroom with basins and running water. In fact the selection on offer is enormous: all you need is money. Naturally the number of extras you get depends upon the amount of money you choose to spend.

For a fee, marquee contractors will also supply the necessary furniture: neat, attractive chairs (often gilt) and round or oblong tables. (Under no circumstances be tempted to save money and borrow these from friends, your local community centre or village hall. An odd assortment of tables, all at different heights, no doubt, will ruin the layout and appearance of the tent, tablecloths will not fit, and stacking chairs will spoil the whole effect.)

If you plan to have floral decorations suspended over-head, make sure the contractors arrange for a pulley *between* the lining and the outer lining. There is also no need at all for poles to be encased in ugly, baggy sleeves. Pole sleeves are designed to fit snugly and should provide a firm and attractive background for flowers and decorations.

The provision and siting of the marquee, together with the decoration, lighting, furniture, food, wine, loos and staff can be undertaken by one of the big party-planning companies. Some offer a brochure; some merely discuss the party with you and 'put something together'. Hand the whole job over to these party people if you wish (and expect to pay handsomely for their services) but insist that the senior partner is on site when the tent goes up. Remember the advice about itemized estimates (see page 21).

Away from home
You can of course be 'At Home' at a club, a restaurant, or

someone else's house – as long as you have sufficient funds, there are lots of places where you will enjoy yourself as much as your guests without having to worry about the crisps running out. (Lists of suitable party headquarters are on pages113-14.)

There are four main categories of 'away' venues for parties: hotels and restaurants; rooms or houses tied to catering companies; friends' homes; and 'unusual' venues.

Entertaining in any hotel seems at first sight rather impersonal. It can also prove to be hideously expensive. However it is true that some very grand hotels do offer a wonderfully efficient service. The choice rests with you and your purse, but whatever the venue watch out for extras such as overtime charges for dismantling decorations after the dance.

Rooms or houses tied to catering companies are often good value, sometimes even better than a catered party at home. (I used Ashton Court Mansion, a beautifully restored house, set in acres of parkland belonging to the Bristol City Council, for my daughter's 21st birthday dance.)

These big houses are geared to catering for crowds. The kitchen facilities function efficiently for large numbers, there are sufficient loos, changing rooms, and plenty of staff on duty to make the party run smoothly. (In our case, they manned the gatehouse, offered excellent security and kept gatecrashers firmly at bay.)

Many companies offering catered rooms and houses are also obliging about wine and allow you to provide your own selection, merely charging corkage on the bottles used – a boon if you're choosy about wines or on good terms with your wine merchant.

On the other hand, borrowing a friend's house can be a big problem. It worked for me once, but basically my advice is *don't*. If you can't refuse the offer, do arrange the loan on a business-like basis. Talk through the plans with your friend and tactfully give her plenty of opportunities to retract her kind offer. Always discuss money: you will, after all, be using her heating and lighting. *Always* take out substantial insurance cover for loss or damage.

As for unusual venues, the possibilities are endless:

boats, cinemas, college halls, livery halls, museums (strictly for non-smokers), art galleries, even disused railway stations, which can make a wonderful venue for a Victorian party, with guests in costume, sipping mulled wine, surrounded by the warm scent of roasting chestnuts.

Charges for unusual venues vary widely. Some can be horrific; others a pleasant surprise. For example, if you are London-based you could have the party to end all parties at the Hippodrome for £40,000. Alternatively a dance in the more haunting setting of Madame Tussaud's may only cost you about £65 a head, including disco. There are no rules; nor, in some cases, precedents. If you want a party somewhere special, the only way to find out the cost is to be brave, pick up the phone and ask.

The best of the professional party organizers (see list on page 115) offer a selection of suitable tried-and-tested unusual venues. But be warned: insist on discussing the costs at your first encounter, however brief that may prove to be.

LIGHTING

While you obviously want pretty, subdued lighting in the main tent, steps, corridors, cloakroom and kitchens must be adequately lit to avoid accidents.

Four types of lighting need to be considered:

(1) general lights: these are best kept quite low to flatter faces; use chandeliers and wall brackets, and ask the contractors for dimmers and spotlights;
(2) high lights: use spotlights or floodlights for the cake, the flowers, the speakers and entertainers; colour co-ordinated candles on each table are pretty too, especially if surrounded by flowers;
(3) special effects: decorative lighting, inside and out, can make a room or tent look magical. Flashing coloured lights at varying speeds, lasers, strobes, coloured patterns and multi-faceted mirror balls all add excitement to dancing. Flood-lit gardens seen through windows help to create a feeling of space. Throw romantic lights on trees, shrubs, statues, waterfalls or ponds. Floodlight the front of your home to welcome guests, provided the façade can stand up

to such attention. For the disco, ask to see a list of the lights the operator expects to provide and check that you have a sufficient supply of power.

(4) practical lighting for the service area: this is a must for safety where people are working and often in a hurry; fluorescent tubes are difficult to adjust to after the dim lighting of the tent, so choose ordinary 100-watt lamps in preference.

From this you will gather that setting the lighting scene is far from simple. Tent contractors will usually organize simple lighting systems (wall lights and central ceiling lights) on site. But for anything more complicated it is best to call in a team of experts. In any event the current needed for a large party may make an unprecedented demand on your domestic power supply; so check with your electrician. He may advise you to hire a portable generator.

MUSIC

You can't have a dance without music and you can't have good music without doing some research. Make a start by considering whether to have a band or a disco or both.

Yet again the decision must depend upon your budget. The facts are that good bands are expensive, but many bad bands cost just as much; discos offer a wider choice and are generally less expensive. In the end, what you need is the right music for the right age group.

A first-class band is worth every pound you spend. An experienced band-leader is not just an expert musician, he's a mind-reader and a barometer too: he can judge the mood of the moment and adapt the tempo and tone of the music accordingly. On the other hand, a bad band takes so many breaks and makes such a grim sound that you might be better off doing a song and dance act yourself.

All musicians expect to be wined and dined equally as well as the guests. But this does not mean you have to endure hours of silence or indifferent filler tapes: very good bands not only play the best music; they bring substitute players so the band never stops. That is why a good band costs so much. If you are thinking of engaging two bands to overcome the gap, my advice is: don't. Changeovers, however well orchestrated, interrupt the carefully-created atmosphere.

When dealing with any type of professional entertainer, a wise party-planner hands over the hassle to a theatrical agent. At the back of this book is a list of well-known agencies which will help you choose suitable musicians, children's entertainers, discos and so on. Not only will the agency staff be extremely helpful, a good agent will arrange a watertight agreement with your chosen artiste, band or disco operator. That way you can safely forget your friends' alarming tales about performers failing to turn up. Musicians will rarely let their agents down but a one-off engagement for a private client might just slip their memory.

Good agents will discuss the party with you, ask about your budget and may suggest a particular band immediately. More normally they will send you details of a selection of artistes and leave the final choice to you. If you plan to engage a band it's worth asking for a demonstration tape. Enquire too about requests: it is important not to find yourself paying for an ego trip, and some bands may try to impose their style on you. Once the booking is made, a deposit is payable directly to the agency, leaving the final account to be settled on the night.

Whatever type of music you arrange, always try to meet the disco operator or band leader about a week ahead of the party. At the very least arrange a chat over the phone. It's important to establish a good working relationship before the party, besides giving yourself an opportunity to iron out any possible difficulties. Discuss numbers, the age of your guests and the general style of the occasion. As a general rule musicians are eager to please, but they can't always guess your favourite music. So discuss the type of music you (and your guests) enjoy. Young people in particular want their special tunes played again and again and often judge a party more by the music than anything else.

No two people agree about the correct level of noise, especially if there's an age difference. Dance music must be fairly loud, otherwise your guests will sit and chat all night. So start the evening with a bang. I recommend you finish that way too: forget about a last waltz grinding the party to a halt. It's better to include one or two slow dances during the evening, but otherwise keep the party going at a steady pace. Atmosphere once created is as fragile as an eggshell.

If you like the idea of alternative dancing, a steel band or a disco in another part of the building is the answer. But bear in mind that this can break up a relatively small dance (under 200 guests) beyond redemption. On the other hand, at a very big ball, the more there is to enjoy, the better.

TABLE PLANS AND PROGRAMMES

Any seating plan worked out in advance must be flexible. Guests may fall ill, emigrate, be overtaken by business commitments, or simply forget to reply until the last minute. Slotting everyone into the right place can be a nightmare. But it's not quite as difficult as it once was, thanks to the invention of magnetic planning boards.

These invaluable boards are available from any good office supplier, together with sheets of magnetic paper, and have almost eradicated last-minute muddles. Invest in one and you can make a table plan in seconds. All you have to do is rule the magnetic card into suitable squares, write the name of each guest in a square, then cut out the named squares and place them along the top of your board. Fitting names to tables then becomes a relatively painless process, and it doesn't matter if, having planned your seating one day, you change your mind completely the next.

When the plan is finished, or as finished as it ever will be, draw up four sets of lists from the board at the last possible moment. Distribute as follows:

(1) one to the printers, for inclusion in the programme if you plan to have one;
(2) one for the caterers: make sure they also have a drawing of the table layout together with relevant table numbers plus stands for the aforesaid numbers;
(3) copies to pin up in the reception area so that guests can see where they are seated;
(4) one for you: even if the caterers put the place names out, the hostess needs to know exactly where everyone is seated.

For a very large dance where a number of attractions are on offer throughout the evening, spread over a wide area, do consider providing a printed programme.

A well-designed programme adds little to the overall cost of the party but contributes greatly to your guests' comfort. The inclusion of a map of the venue (if necessary) and a timetable also allows guests to know the form in advance and plan their evening. It is such a shame to find too late that you missed the cabaret, or failed to discover the disco, never mind losing out on the breakfast. Other useful notices can be printed inside a programme too: where to find first-aid assistance, arrangements in case of fire, and general security measures taken.

Finally, remember that an attractive programme provides the perfect souvenir for a special evening. Your guests will keep it for years to come.

Use the ordering technique suggested for printed invitations on page 17.

SECURITY

Some people do extraordinary things to get into parties. They lie, cheat, steal, forge invitations or simply walk in. Sadly, in many circles, a certain amount of gatecrashing seems to be almost inevitable. If this is the case in your set, all you can do is take sensible security precautions. One solution, particularly useful when dealing with large crowds of young people, is to supply all *bona fide* guests with wrist tags, or simply stamp their wrists with a rubber stamp – a long-established practice at university dances. Should a few uninvited guests appear despite your best efforts, under no circumstances allow their presence to disturb you. Evidence of your displeasure will only add to their entertainment. Ignore them instead, or organize their swift expulsion from a distance. *Never* become embroiled in an argument with uninvited guests at your own party.

Gatecrashers apart, it is an unfortunate fact that parties for large numbers always represent a security risk. Your home, normally tranquil and secure, suddenly becomes a vulnerable playground for boisterous guests and – worse – a treasure trove, ripe for easy pickings. It takes only a few seconds for a hooligan to wreck a room or slip away with the family silver. You may hate the idea but the only real way to minimize the risk is to engage the experts: a professional security firm.

Discuss your party on site with a representative of the security firm, who will be in a position to point out the vulnerable areas in your home and suggest ways to prevent trouble.

The duties you can expect security staff to undertake normally include checking invitations at the door, and thereafter dealing with drunks, uninvited guests and prowlers. But if you have a large country home they will also check on the more deserted areas of your house and grounds.

If you plan to use a swimming pool at the party, it is imperative that someone with a recognized life-saving qualification is in attendance *all the time.*

For any big event complete insurance cover is a must. If you have to cancel the party at the last minute the policy will at least take care of the costs incurred. Likewise should an accident occur or a thief strike, you will be covered. Consult your insurance broker, who will be pleased to arrange adequate protection.

ENDING IT ALL

Some people will stay on and dance all night if you let them, particularly the 18- to 25-year-olds. How to get guests to leave without giving offence can be a problem. One solution is to state the finishing as well as the starting time on the invitation ('8 p.m. till midnight'): another is to adopt the Victorian system and write 'Carriages at 11 o'clock' on the invitation, thereby indicating the end of the proceedings.

In a hotel or restaurant, the current licensing laws impose a natural limit on the length of your party. Even at home it is wise to finish on a high note rather than grind to a juddering halt halfway through the night. Never mind shouts of 'Shame!' from the younger, more enthusiastic partygoers: your helpers will certainly appreciate the opportunity to get home to bed at a reasonable hour.

The only really effective way to draw the party to a close is to stop serving food and drink. If you have a band or

disco, ask them to announce that the last number will be
. . . (whatever), then play something suitable after which
they announce, 'That's it, goodnight, everyone.' For a
small occasion you could try shouting, 'Time to go home,
you lot' (it has been known) or turning on the lights; or you
might go to bed yourself. Whatever tactics you adopt, do
not expect determined hangers-on to be discouraged by
your actions – they will surely stay until there is nothing at
all left to drink.

CHAPTER 3

Dinner parties

One of the nicest ways to make friends and influence people is to give a good dinner party. 'Dinner party', in this context, has nothing at all to do with informal gatherings around the kitchen table – quite the reverse: this chapter is about getting out the best china, glassware and linen and having a meal to match. It is about enjoying a drink and conversation without last-minute panics in the kitchen. More important, the aim is to help you help others to relax in your home.

The secret of a successful dinner party does not lie in the provision of elaborate food and elegant decoration, but in how well people get on with each other.

People make a good dinner party in precisely the same way as they make or mar any other type of party, only more so. Get the mixture right and you will all have a wonderful evening. Get it wrong and the meal is doomed to grind on relentlessly from the starter to the cheese, with no escape route for anyone.

All dinner parties need to be planned and prepared in advance. The more work you put into a party beforehand, the more your guests – and you – are likely to enjoy it. Six friends, plenty of hope and nothing much in the fridge is a recipe for disaster.

The ideal time to start planning a dinner party is about three or four weeks ahead. Take the necessary decisions and draw up a series of lists to cover the guests, the food and the wine. Write out a shopping list and a timetable, itemizing every job. Plan to cook ahead as much as possible and use every available modern convenience to lessen the workload. Microwaves, freezers and ready-prepared foods all come into their own at a dinner party.

Moral for a cook/hostess: get organized in advance and

stay organized. That way you will be calmly confident.

CHOOSING AND INVITING GUESTS

How many? Much depends upon the size of your dining table. The very best dinner parties are probably *à deux* with someone special. After that it is a matter of taste.

Attempting to cater unaided for more than ten people is plainly daft. The object of the exercise is to be *with* your guests, not to spend all night dashing to and from the kitchen. A flustered. over-busy hostess makes her guests feel guilty and uncomfortable.

Whom to ask? Be ruthless. Invite only the people you really want. Aim for a thorough mix: mix brains with beauty, wit with charm, solicitors with salesmen, accountants with scriptwriters, editors with boat-builders. Mix professions, nationalities and ages.

Apart from purely business dinner parties, never invite anyone because you have to. Fit the neighbours and boring Mrs Bloggs in at some giant drinks-only affair. Your carefully prepared food (and that means your time and money) are too precious to waste.

Whenever possible avoid having a party made up solely of couples. A fascinating woman often has a boring husband – or the other way round. Interesting, talented, single people, from any age group, add sparkle to a dinner party.

For dinner parties the telephone invitation is both quick and practical. People can then tell you at once whether they can come. They can also tell you their important news and warn you if they are slimming or on a special diet.

If you're planning a party around someone in particular, telephone him or her first. Suggest one or two dates, two or three weeks ahead. The exact amount of notice you need to offer depends, to a large extent, upon your circle of friends and the day of the week. Friday and Saturday nights tend to get booked up quickly: people go away or have friends to stay. If prospective guests are too busy on both suggested occasions do not pester them. Instead, politely turn the conversation to other things and say you'll get in touch another time.

When you invite strangers to your house for the first

time, it is courteous to follow up the phone call with a brief note of confirmation, giving your exact address and phone number, as well as details about time and what to wear. It is also a good idea to enclose a map or at least clear directions about how to reach your home, particularly if you live in the depths of the country.

Americans and a few efficient English businessmen send a list and short biography of other guests to each member of the party. That way social seeds are sown and social blunders avoided. If the idea appeals to you, draw up a single sheet of brief, simple information in advance and post just before the party.

PLANNING THE MENU

The ambition of every dinner party host or hostess should be to have the guests depart reluctantly, rather later than they should, but still feeling great. What you do not want is for them to totter off the doorstep over-fed, exhausted and slightly tipsy.

The trick is not to be mean with the drink, but rather to be extremely careful with the food.

It is the combination of too much rich food coupled with alcohol that is frequently responsible for the 'morning-after' feeling. Even if you sip only mineral water all night, you can be horribly hung-over after a meal of Camembert with gooseberry sauce, honey-baked ham and crème caramel, as each course contains a higher-than-average amount of fat.

That is not to say you should omit anything that is rich and fun to eat. Just keep a sense of balance. The inclusion of eggs, alcohol and cream in every course will only succeed in giving your guests indigestion.

'Keep it simple' may be a cliché, but it's well worth remembering. Granny's advice about 'knowing your limitations' is also very sound. But cooking for a dinner party should be an enjoyable exercise, so give yourself some room to experiment and have some fun.

Once you decide upon a menu, stick to it. Provided that the rest of the meal is good, the occasional failure will not mar your reputation. I once threw a complete cake in the dustbin at five minutes to eight: the sugar had been forgotten, among other things. Nobody minded going without pudding; in fact, we all had a good laugh – people secretly enjoy the occasional failure: it breaks the ice like nothing else and has the odd effect of putting people at their ease.

However, this book is supposed to put you on the track for success, so here are a few ways to ensure just that . . .

Remember, it's style that makes meals memorable. The food should look and taste good, and present a picture of elegant simplicity.

Count on serving three courses, plus cheese and coffee. A hot dish sandwiched between two cold ones works best for the cook/hostess.

Cook ahead and minimize any last-minute work. When selecting a recipe, make sure you read every stage through carefully and decide for yourself how much last-minute bother you can cope with: only you know if you can manage in the time available.

Use herbs and spices with care. Not everyone is crazy about garlic – or mint, for that matter. *Never* serve curry without an alternative unless you are quite certain about your guests' tastes.

Provide a selection of good, fresh, lightly cooked vegetables. In an emergency remember that a pastry brush dipped in melted butter can put a shine on tired-looking vegetables.

Make a pudding that no one in their right minds could resist.

Only Superwoman or the romantic lead in a Hollywood film can whisk up a delicious dinner while guests hang around the kitchen, glass in hand. In real life the best dinner parties are those where the cooking has been done in advance.

Special considerations
Don't forget that some people cannot eat certain foods, for a whole range of reasons. Guests may be allergic to specific foods or restricted to special diets for health reasons, in which case they will usually warn their hostess in advance.

Consideration must be given to religious beliefs, too:

strict Roman Catholics may prefer not to eat meat on Fridays; Jews and Muslims are forbidden pork, and Jews do not mix meat and dairy products in the same meal. Muslims are not allowed alcohol. Diabetics must not have sugar, so fresh fruit or cheese should be on offer to substitute for a sugary dessert. And many people nowadays are trying to keep their fat intake in check, so go easy on the cream and butter.

Vegetarians do not eat meat (or fish either, in many cases) but enjoy a certain amount of dairy produce. In effect this means acceptable dishes include those made from milk, eggs, cheese, butter, vegetables, pulses, fruit, cereals and nuts. Vegans, on the other hand, eat no animal products at all. Food for this group must therefore be carefully planned in advance. As a general rule, suitable dishes are those made from cereals, pulses, nuts and vegetables.

There are some very good vegetarian cookery books available to inspire you if you are faced with this problem, most of which include a few vegan recipes. Your local health food store may also be able to give you some ideas.

Dinner parties can be a problem for people who are trying to lose weight, too. As the host or hostess, try to help a little if you can. Don't fall into the trap of thinking that small portions are mean. Many people prefer them. Attempting to force-feed people who are obviously trying to cut down their food intake is pushy and rude, no matter how long it took you to make the pudding. Avoid offering slimmers second helpings, if you can. Don't take offence if some people actually prefer to eat nothing and, if possible, provide a selection of cold meats or plain foods for dieters. A dish of hard-boiled eggs nestling in a bed of crisp lettuce is not a difficult extra to supply. Serve salad dressings separately. Dieters can then eat their lettuce plain, or nibble unadorned grated carrot or carrot sticks with a clear conscience.

Have a stock of low-calorie tonics and plenty of mineral water to offer weight-watchers. Drivers will welcome these too. Remember to offer sweeteners and skimmed milk if you serve coffee. Sugar and cream are now virtually *passé* in many circles.

Drinks

An aperitif before a meal is intended to stimulate both the palate and the appetite. The choice offered to guests before dinner is therefore just as important as the choice of wines to accompany your carefully selected food.

Purists and wine buffs normally prefer dry (*fino*) sherry, dry (*sercial*) madeira, dry vermouth or a light dry white wine. Champagne is always a good choice. Most people enjoy a glass or two and it is easy to organize and serve.

You should also offer gin (with tonic), whisky (with soda or mineral water) and medium dry sherry. Sweet sherry and sticky cocktails all deaden the tastebuds and dull the appetite, and are therefore best avoided before a meal.

Until recently, many people felt unable to admit their preference for soft drinks, as it almost certainly meant they would be labelled 'odd'. Now it is perfectly acceptable to drink little or no alcohol. The thoughtful hostess recognizes the need to sustain the abstainer and offers a selection of soft drinks: carbonated mineral water, freshly squeezed orange juice (the two mixed are very refreshing), as well as diet cola. In addition many non-alcoholic wines and lagers are now widely available.

Your choice of wines to be served during dinner will depend on the menu. White wine is generally served with the fish course, while red wine accompanies the meat course, with a sweet white wine to complement the dessert, and port to finish. You can of course be flexible and take into account your own and your guests' tastes. For more detailed advice, see pages 28-30.

THE DINNER TABLE

A beautifully-laid table is universally admired. The trouble is that creating a look of *grand luxe* takes time. This is fine if you have help. If not, there are plenty of things you can do the night before the party.

Set the table. (If your house is open-plan, stack the necessary items on a tray ready to place in position next day.) Polish cutlery and glasses till they gleam. Be sure you have the correct implements for each course: for example, fish with lots of bones needs both knives and forks. Betjeman sneered at the fish knives introduced by the practical Victorians. Follow the poet's lead if you must, but do provide some sort of knife.

Check that you have enough china for each course. (This sounds obvious but is overlooked surprisingly often.) If not, borrow from a kind friend and make a note to buy more as soon as possible. If you do not have a matching dinner service invest in one as soon as possible. It need not be expensive. Go for simplicity: plain white china or white with a gold or coloured band is the most stylish.

Make sure you have sufficient spotlessly clean cloth napkins, which should be folded and placed on the side plate on the left of the place setting. White napkins look lovely against polished wood. Napkin rings are never used at dinner parties (nor should they be used at any other occasion – they're an unhygienic relic of days long gone, when napkins were used again and again before they were laundered).

Consider the lighting; it is almost more important than the flowers. Never have overhead lights. Light directed down on to a dinner table will give all the guests, of every age group, bags under the eyes and four chins. Wall lights or table lamps are much kinder. Candlelight is even better and much more romantic; but there must be enough candles. No one likes groping about in the dark for food.

When you lay the table, avoid the temptation to over-decorate. If you have a beautifully polished table, why cover it up with a cloth? Use matching mats which allow your guests to see the gleaming wood. If you're not lucky enough to have a beautiful table then use a pretty tablecloth with matching napkins.

Napkins

Some clever people like to fold napkins into interesting shapes, such as lilies or cones. The easiest shape to master, however, is the mitre. Practise a few times with newspaper cut to size, rather than spoil freshly starched napkins. Here's how:

(1) Take the napkin and fold it in half, then in half again.
(2) Fold it again, this time diagonally. Bring the two base points of the triangle together and slip one inside the other.

Cutlery

People are sometimes daunted by the prospect of laying up a three- or four-course place setting. Where should you put so many knives and forks? The answer is simple. Imagine you are seated at the table and place everything according to the course, working from the outside (for the first course) inwards.

If, for example, you propose to serve soup, fish, meat and then dessert, first place the small butter knife on the right-hand side at a distance from the plate, followed by the soup spoon, the fish knife, larger meat knife, and, nearest the plate, the dessert spoon.

On the left side of the plate, again working from the outside, place first the fish fork, then the meat fork and finally, nearest the plate, the dessert fork.

While in theory all place settings should be laid out as suggested, it is acceptable to adapt these rules to suit your table and the meal you propose to serve. Some people prefer to place the dessert spoon and fork above the plates – the spoon pointing to the left above the fork which should point to the right. Similarly, if space is limited, place the butter knife on the side plate. In a severely restricted eating area you may be obliged to omit the side plate and butter knife altogether; in this case, serve buttered toast or bread and put the starter on slightly larger plates.

Glassware

For a large drinks party, inexpensive glasses can be borrowed or hired from your local wine merchant; for a dinner party, however, your own set of special glasses will look best. If you're lucky enough to have crystal, use it. If not, most stores sell reasonably priced glass in boxes of six or eight. Give yourself a present: a good set of glasses, kept strictly for dinner parties, is a worthwhile investment. Make sure you buy glass all of the same type: the port, sherry, white wine and claret glasses must match. A mixture of odd glassware makes a table look messy.

Wine buffs disapprove of cut crystal and insist that plain glass shows fine wines to their best advantage. This may be the case, but beautifully cut crystal glasses gleaming in the candlelight add extra sparkle to a dinner table. Whichever type of glass you choose, wash it with care and store separately from your everyday glass. A good set of glass can last for years.

In a formal dinner party a different wine is offered with each course. Here's a guide to help avoid confusion:

(1) sherry glass – for the soup course;
(2) white wine glass – for the fish course;
(3) red wine glass – for the meat course;
(4) dessert wine glass (same size as the dry white wine glass);
(5) port glass;
(6) tumbler – for mineral water.

Before or after the meal you might also use champagne glasses, cocktail glasses and brandy balloons.

One way to tell at a glance which glass to use for which wine is to remember that the shapes are all based on common sense. Sherry is a strong fortified wine and is therefore served in a small glass. White wine is normally cold, so the glass has a long stem to prevent the warmth of the hand taking the chill away, while the bowl of the red wine glass is plump and comfortable to nestle in the hand and allow you the opportunity to appreciate the 'nose'.

Just as with the cutlery, you place the glass on the table working from the outside in, according to which wine is to be taken with which course. It may seem at first sight like a lot of fuss and even more washing-up; but you really cannot change wines and drink from the same glass. Not only would the taste be impaired but the bouquet and freshness of the wine would almost certainly be lost. Besides, it is not graceful to ask guests to drink up their white wine while you brandish bottles of claret.

On the other hand, few of us are likely to provide a battery of glassware and comprehensive array of wine at a private dinner party. A crisp dry white wine with the first course followed by a good red wine is the normal arrangement. Even so, some people do not enjoy red wine and prefer to stick to white throughout the meal. On special occasions it's fun to introduce a sweet white wine or even a glass of medium champagne to accompany the dessert.

Always provide a tumbler for mineral water. If you are entertaining a foreign guest, who may not be accustomed to drinking wine, put a slice of lemon in the tumbler to avoid confusion about the contents of the other glasses.

Flowers

One graceful arrangement of flowers adds style to a dinner-party table. The trick is to keep your arrangement *small*. No one wants to eat in the midst of a botanical garden, or have to duck and dive in order to see the person sitting opposite.

Ensure that the colours of the flowers blend with your cloth (if you use one), china and general décor. Always think first and buy second. Allow the size and shape of your table to influence the design of your decoration, for example, a circular arrangement for a round table.

Choose flowers that are in season and therefore at their best. Make sure both flowers and foliage are absolutely fresh: flowers that have seen better days will have a deadening effect on any party. In winter, when even a few fresh flowers cost a small fortune, use silk or dried flowers instead. Both offer good value for money. Remove dust from silk flowers with a hairdrier. Some can even be swished clean in warm soapy water, using washing-up liquid.

Take care of your flowers. Give both bought or garden flowers a long drink (put them in cold water right up to their necks) for at least an hour before arranging them. Buy cut flowers two days ahead in bud. Cut away the first two inches of the stem before you put them in water. Keep all flowers in a cool place, particularly once arranged in oasis. Spray arrangements with a fine mist of water at regular intervals. Flowers absorb water through their petals as well as through their stems.

For a stunning oval table, use a pale green cloth covered with a white lace cloth, pale green napkins, dark green candles, and two small posies of tiny white roses with glossy dark leaves.

A pretty fresh-flower arrangement from your local florist can be surprisingly inexpensive and will save precious time when you are under pressure.

Seating plans

There are four simple rules for seating guests at a formal dinner party:

(1) the host and hostess sit at opposite ends of the table;
(2) the most important male guest sits on the right of the hostess; the second most important man sits to her left;
(3) the most important female guest sits on the right of the host, the second most important to his left;
(4) husbands and wives are best separated.

However, rules are made to be broken. The shape of your table and the number of guests will be the strongest influence on your seating plan.

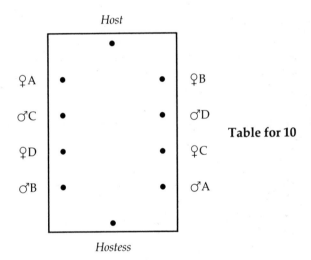

From the illustration you will see that to follow the man/woman/man pattern around the table the host and hostess can only sit at opposite ends of the table when there are 6, 10, 14, 16 or 18 people at the table.

So how should you seat eight? In our home, we use the 'women in the corners' technique (see illustration). You may prefer to leave the hostess's end of the table unchanged and rearrange the host's end.

Another exception to the rule is that, for some inexplicable reason, at some official functions husbands are always seated next to their wives.

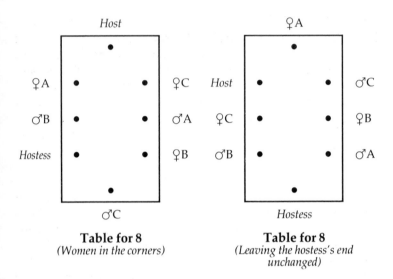

Table for 8
(*Women in the corners*)

Table for 8
(*Leaving the hostess's end
unchanged*)

A bride takes precedence over any woman, other than a member of the royal family. A bride remains a bride, according to the etiquette books, for six months after the marriage ceremony. So when it is your turn, make the most of it.

For small dinner parties of eight or ten it is the duty of the hostess to lead her guests into dinner and tell them where to sit.

However, hieroglyphics scribbled on the back of the hand, which cannot be deciphered at the moment of truth, do nothing for the serene hostess image. Trying to remember, unaided, a carefully worked-out seating scheme is equally hopeless. A much better idea is to make yourself a plan to help you tell people where to sit. Even better, make two copies, as ideally both the host and hostess should know the seating arrangements in advance.

For large, formal dinner parties it is best to write out place names or put china name plates at each seat so that everyone knows where they should be.

You can buy smart, white, gold-edged place cards at good stationers, and pretty china name plates in large department stores.

ON THE NIGHT

The normal hour to be invited for dinner is 8 p.m., but you can vary this to suit yourself and your guests. Those with babysitters may prefer an earlier start, those with business commitments some distance away a later one. Whatever time you choose, allow three-quarters of an hour *only* for drinks before you sit down to dinner. The American and Spanish custom of two hours' solid drinking before a meal is not only barbaric, it is unfair to the cook... especially if that's you.

If guests arrive late, that is their misfortune: they get just one drink instead of two or three. Most people can be on time if they make an effort and will at least arrive within 45 minutes. Traffic hold-ups or train delays may be unavoidable, but a quick call to alert the hostess is almost always possible.

Once guests arrive it is up to you to make them feel comfortable and at ease. So offer guests a drink first, then introduce them to each other and if necessary help to get the conversation going.

In most instances the pre-dinner period sets the tone for evening. So be attentive to your guests' needs. Notice and top up any empty glasses – many people swallow their first drink with surprising speed. Keep an eye open to make sure no one is left out or cornered by a bore. Similarly, try to avoid a situation where people whom you intend to sit next to each other get stuck together during the pre-dinner drinks. They may have nothing left to talk about during the meal.

On no account greet guests with a brief 'Hello', hand them a drink and then hurry away to hide in the kitchen. It's rude. Prepare the food before your friends arrive (or get some help with the cooking).

At the appointed time the hostess leads the party into dinner. The women follow her and are in turn closely followed by the men. As everyone reaches the table it is up to the hostess to indicate where people should sit.

Creating the right ambiance

Making guests feel wanted and welcome at your party is infinitely more important than subscribing to convention, so don't worry too much about the rules of etiquette when entertaining at home. Mixing guests so that they have an opportunity to get to know each other is an art which cannot properly be prescribed in any book. The experienced host appears to work by instinct. In fact, the secret of successful introductions is to relax and to concentrate on giving pleasure to your guests.

The first five minutes at a party are often the most difficult, particularly for shy people, so it is vitally important that you welcome guests warmly on arrival and look after their immediate needs. Find them their first drink. Introduce them to some like-minded people. Tell them a little about each other, to help them start a conversation on common ground.

Recognizing your friends' foibles can also be a great help. Some people enjoy making conversation, while for others small talk is torture. This is yet another reason to plan the guest list with care: including several good mixers who will join in the party unaided will allow you more time to spend with shy friends who need to relax before being led gently towards sympathetic souls.

If you wish to invite a famous or important person to your party, be sure you know him or her sufficiently well. Most VIPs hate to be used on a rent-a-star basis (charity appearances are an exception). On the other hand, if you are very friendly with a celebrity, do not let his or her exalted position deter you from offering your hospitality. Celebrities enjoy parties just like everyone else.

However, it is true that famous people often draw a crowd of people round them at parties. Some, particularly politicians, like the attention. Others hate it, or enjoy it for a short time only. Be aware of the situation and rescue your friend should the need occur.

If you have a member of the royal family as a guest at your party, remember that other guests may be shy or reluctant to appear forward. It is your duty to bring people to speak to your important guest and see that a great divide does not open up across the room, leaving your royal guest separated from the rest of the party.

There are two very simple rules to follow when making an introduction:

(1) Introduce men to women on all occasions: 'John, do come and meet Jane.' In the same way, introduce the junior to the senior – for example, the captain to the colonel: 'Colonel Blythe, do you know Captain Jones?'
(2) Speak up and don't mumble.

Titles can be a problem. Most people do not use them on purely social occasions, but in a formal setting it is best to be perfectly correct. If you don't know the form, look it up in *Burke's Peerage* or *Debrett* (find both in your local reference library), which give clear guidance on the subject.

In addition there is another group of people who are not listed in *Burke's* or *Debrett* but who none the less expect to be addressed correctly. This list may help:

- Admirals, Rear-Admirals and Vice-Admirals are all called 'Admiral'.
- Generals, Major-Generals and Lieutenant-Generals are all called 'General'.
- Air Marshals, Air Vice-Marshals, Air Commodores and Group Captains are all called by their individual titles.
- Surgeons should always be called 'Mister', never 'Doctor'.
- Judges are addressed as 'Mr Justice Brown', although in practice many have knighthoods or have been raised to the peerage, in which case see *Debrett* and use their title.
- Doctors are called 'Doctor' or 'Doctor Brown'.
- Vicars should be addressed as 'Vicar' or 'Mr Brown', never 'Reverend Brown'. Modern clergy often prefer to be called by their Christian names.
- Lord Mayors are always addressed as 'Lord Mayor' in conversation, whether male or female.

Ideally, conversation at a dinner party should be a polite, interesting, witty discussion – not a heated argument. This does not of course mean you have to be a milk-and-water person. If you feel strongly about an issue, say so – but aim to express your opinion without making others look foolish, lose face or feel uncomfortable.

It may sound like a counsel of perfection, but do try to be tactful if you disagree with someone. Politeness costs nothing and people who consistently dominate the conversation are never the most popular.

Rich and famous personages often like to hold the stage at dinner parties. This does not usually matter since most people will be quite interested to hear their views. However, some are so conceited they slip up: one well-known millionaire lectured a dear friend of ours (master vintner and wine connoisseur) for over an hour about the man's *own* château-bottled wine. The moral of the story might be: find out a bit about the person sitting next to you before launching into your own pet subject.

Boring people to death with the technical aspects of your job, about which they know little and care even less, is another social sin. The trouble is that natural enthusiasm sometimes overcomes sensitivity: a journalist friend of ours, when suddenly promoted, once talked endlessly about her work at a dinner party without realizing that everyone stopped listening after a while. You can put your friends' minor obsessions into context; other guests may not be so understanding.

So what *can* you talk about? Almost anything: books, theatre, television, parties, people, animals, gardening... even the weather if you really can't think of anything else. More obscure subjects can add variety but avoid blinding your audience with science. It is also fine to talk about commonplace things like carpets, camping or cooking, and even politics or religion shouldn't be taboo – just as long as you stay cool.

On the other hand things you should *not* talk about under any circumstances are: money – particularly other people's – or the tax system; last night's/week's party (how rude!); family differences or your partner's peculiar habits (no one wants to know); children and their education (a bore for childless couples); your brand-new compact disc-player, personal computer, microwave, dish-washer, or other tedious domestic acquisitions. *Never* indulge in malicious gossip, make sneering comments or constantly criticize anyone or anything.

Bear in mind that compulsive talking is an affliction of the shy and nervous – stay calm to avoid succumbing to such an attack yourself. After all, the most tiresome man (or woman) in the world is the one who, when asked, 'How are you?', tells all.

How to serve dinner
There seems to be a good deal of confusion about how to serve food at dinner parties. Many people are unsure whether to serve all the female guests first. There's the worry about which side food should be served from. What happens about the wine is another problem. Does the hostess mean what she says when she urges, 'Do start'? And what about the cheese . . . should it come before the dessert or after?

The answer to these and most other problems connected with entertaining is more a matter of using your common sense and doing what is practical in your home rather than following convention. But here are a few guidelines which may help.

The correct way to serve food, whether you have helpers or not, is to start with the most important female guest and go round the table anti-clockwise – a simple and practical solution which allows any accompanying dishes to be passed smoothly round the table. The idea of serving all the women first is impractical and silly.

Wherever space allows, and in all formal situations, food is served from the left. Wine is poured from the right.

At formal dinner parties where there are waiters, guests should not start eating until everyone has been served. When entertaining at home, a wise cook/hostess urges guests to begin when they are served hot food. Guests should not disregard her request, but should start to eat and enjoy her food while it is hot.

Make sure each course is completely cleared away before the next is served. Allow a few minutes' gap between a light first course and the main dish. When the main course has been eaten, allow a short pause for people to savour their wine and chat before you bring on the dessert or cheese.

English practice is to serve the pudding before the

cheese; in France the cheese is offered first. Which you do at your dinner parties is a matter of personal choice. Smoking during a meal is always anti-social, wherever you are.

If you serve port after dinner, place the decanter on the table for guests to help themselves. Port is always passed from right to left. Offer good, freshly made coffee either at the table or in the drawing room.

How to eat difficult foods

It is an uncomfortable fact that there are certain foods which are difficult to eat with any elegance. There are also a number of less familiar foods, exotic fruits in particular, which may give cause for panic at first sight. A wise hostess considers both points when planning a menu.

Some foods are best avoided altogether in a formal context: small birds such as quail or pigeon, because guests will be unwilling to pick up the bones in their fingers, and corn on the cob and spaghetti, both of which can be eaten only at the expense of elegance and are therefore better served on more relaxed occasions.

On the other hand, asparagus and globe artichokes (both of which have to be picked up by the hand) are very acceptable, though rather messy (a mere matter of convention, you might think, and you may be right).

The following list should help you plan effectively and avoid the worst pitfalls:

Artichokes (globe) Begin at the outside. Tear off one leaf at a time. Dip the fleshy white tip of each leaf into the accompanying butter and then bite it off. Pile the used leaves on the side of the plate. The leaves near the heart of the artichoke are more transparent and have no taste. Pile these up uneaten to expose the heart. Scrape away the thistle at the base of the artichoke and then eat the heart with a knife and fork. Finger bowls are normally provided with artichokes.

Asparagus Pick up by the white end and dip the green tip in the accompanying butter or sauce. Then gradually bite off the green part all the way down to the lower part where the green turns white. Finally lay the white stem neatly on the side of the plate.

Use the finger bowl to rinse your fingers.

Banana   Prince Charles apparently eats a banana with a knife and fork. If you find his example too difficult to follow, at least cut the peeled fruit into bite-sized portions. Who wants to look like a monkey at the dining table?

Figs, fresh (green or purply-black)   Use a knife to remove the stalk and cut the fruit into bite-sized sections. Both flesh and seeds are eaten. Peeling is not usually necessary.

Fish   Sole, mackerel, trout and mullet are often served unfilleted. Remove any skin with your knife, eat the upper side of the fish, then remove the spine and bones and tackle the rest. When you eat a sole cut away the fringe bone round the edge. Run your knife down the centre of the fish from top to tail and eat both fillets before removing the spine and eating the rest.

Guava   A pear-shaped tropical fruit from Brazil with a pale yellow-green skin and pink flesh, which is used mostly in fruit salads but can be eaten raw. Cut a small piece from each end, then cut into quarters. Use a spoon to scoop up the pinkish-white flesh with edible white seeds.

Kumquat   Originally grown in China, the kumquat is a small, oval, orange-coloured citrus fruit with a thin, edible rind and a sweet/tart taste. Eat it whole with your fingers. Do not peel.

Lychees   Fresh lychees are small and round with brittle, reddish-brown skins. The flesh is white, juicy and tangy. When the fruit is ripe it should 'give' slightly when pressed. To eat, peel away the shell and eat the sweet, perfumed flesh inside. Use your fingers.

Mango   There are hundreds of varieties of mango but those most often encountered at dinner parties are the non-fibrous dessert variety. The skin colours range from yellow-green to dark crimson. A mango must be ripe to eat and should always be prepared in the kitchen. Cut away the flesh from the large flat stone by slicing down one side as close as possible and repeating on the other side. Trim off any remaining flesh. Make criss-cross cuts through the flesh in a square pattern. Bend back the flesh. The delicious cubes of mango can then be eaten using a spoon or fork.

Oysters   Usually presented on a bed of cracked ice,

oysters are eaten from the half shell with a squeeze of fresh lemon juice. Balance the slippery flesh on a fork and swallow whole.

Passion fruit   Plum-sized, with hard, brownish skin, the ripe passion fruit looks like a shrivelled plum. The flesh is yellow and juicy; the seeds are edible. To eat at the table, cut in half and use a teaspoon to scoop out the fresh, tangy flesh.

Pawpaw/papaya   A sub-tropical, pear-shaped fruit with smooth, yellowish-green skin, pink flesh and numerous dark seeds, the pawpaw is normally prepared in the kitchen, where the inedible seeds can be removed with ease. Eat with a teaspoon as you would an avocado pear; or, if it is served peeled and prepared in strips, use a fork.

Persimmon (called **kaki fruit** if from Italy, and **sharon fruit** if from Israel)   The fruit resembles an angular, yellow-orange tomato with a large green cap. It has sweet flesh, no seeds and an edible skin. To eat it at the table, cut in half and scoop out flesh with a teaspoon.

Pomegranate   About the size of a large orange, this fruit has hard, golden-red outer skin, which contains numerous juicy red seeds. A great favourite with children and best left for them to enjoy, seed by seed.

Snails   These are usually served with special eating implements: tongs and a narrow fork. Hold the shell with the tongs and winkle the whole snail out with your fork. Mop up the delicious butter sauce with small pieces of bread if you wish. (This does not mean you should behave like a French peasant and wipe the plate clean.)

After dinner

Whether to expect the women to withdraw to the drawing room (or wherever) after the meal is a vexed question. Once upon a time, convention ruled and everyone knew the form: womenfolk were expected to retire and leave the men to enjoy their port at the table. Happily this irritating custom has all but died out.

However it must be said that a change of scenery can sometimes bring a dull dinner guest to life or at least give his or her long-suffering neighbours a chance to chat to someone else. The solution may be for the women to enjoy a glass of port and then make a move to leave the men at the table. If the ladies do withdraw, it is up to the host to see that the men make a move to join them at an early stage: fifteen minutes is quite long enough.

It's a good idea, if you live in town, to ask other friends to join you for after-dinner drinks and coffee. Invite people who have been to the theatre or the cinema to come along afterwards. New faces and fresh conversation add an extra late-night sparkle to your dinner party.

Preventing last-minute panics

If you are entertaining after a day at work, have a long cool drink when you get home before you do anything – that way you can slow down and make a mental plan of campaign. If you've planned efficiently and written everything down, the going will be easier.

Do whatever you have to do in the kitchen but leave yourself time to dress up. A steamy, flustered cook will not put guests at their ease and could make them feel guilty.

Be ready to welcome the guests on arrival; then hand over gracefully to the host while you finalize the kitchen arrangements. (Make your absence only a matter of minutes.) That way you won't appear to have disappeared and the meal will appear almost by magic.

Bon appetit!

CHAPTER 4

Informal entertaining

More and more entertaining at home is done on an informal basis. Everyone enjoys the freedom of seeing friends in a relaxed atmosphere. However, 'informal' should not mean second-rate food and rough red wine. Neither should it mean forgetting all you ever knew about lighting, decoration and planning.

Informal entertaining means organizing a party where the food is simple, the setting and the atmosphere relaxed, and where your guests complete the picture by dressing in casual clothes.

Such parties can be held both in your house and out of doors and include brunch parties, kitchen suppers, after-theatre suppers, afternoon tea and barbecues. In this chapter you will find lots of help to make your informal entertaining both successful and enjoyable.

BRUNCH
This is an American idea that has gained popularity virtually worldwide. It's easy to see why. There's no need to get up at dawn for a start and no need for suits or high heels: just comfortable weekend casual gear and no hassle.

The best thing about brunch (a combination of breakfast and lunch, usually eaten towards the end of the morning) is that this type of entertaining provides the perfect opportunity to meet friends and enjoy a long, leisurely meal without working your fingers to the bone. Once brunch is over, everyone, including the cook, is free to enjoy a walk, swim or play tennis during the afternoon.

Invite six or eight good friends by phone about a week ahead, and ask your guests to arrive at about eleven in the morning. Welcome them with a glass of Buck's Fizz or straight champagne.

Aim to serve the meal between 11.30 a.m. and noon. Remember that your guests may have had only a cup of coffee since they got up so they are likely to be quite hungry.

When you plan the menu, select food which can be prepared the previous evening. As always, cook ahead as far as possible and make full use of your freezer and microwave oven.

It's fun in winter to serve brunch in the dining room, the sideboard spread with goodies under high Edwardian covers. Alternatively you might prefer to be in the kitchen, particularly if yours is a large one complete with old-fashioned dresser. In high summer, brunch is perfect outside: the meal will be over before the sun gets too hot. In fact, it doesn't matter very much where you serve brunch. What matters is that the surroundings are bright and cheerful and that the food is fresh and hot.

Serve fresh fruit to start and then offer a choice of three main dishes. Here are a few ideas to help you plan:

- Scrambled eggs with smoked salmon stirred into them or mixed with little pieces of crispy bacon. In both cases get the ingredients ready the night before and cook just before serving.
- Bacon-wrapped sausages: use chipolatas and bake in the oven. If you have an automatic timer, the sausages will cook almost by magic. Lightly grill the bacon, wrap round the sausages and return them to a low oven to keep warm.
- Kedgeree: make it overnight and warm up in the morning.
- Crispy salmon fish cakes: make them days ahead and store in the freezer. Cook just before the guests arrive.
- A selection of prepared but uncooked rolls, muffins, waffles, all from the freezer. Good supermarkets stock these.
- Some high-quality jam – home-made if possible.
- Piles of fresh fruit.
- Real coffee and perhaps hot chocolate, sprinkled with cinnamon.

Guests help themselves to food and drink.

AFTERNOON TEA

Essentially a British meal, the fashion for afternoon tea began in the early part of the nineteenth century when Anna, Duchess of Bedford, unable to beat the pangs of mid-afternoon hunger, ordered a pot of tea and some snacks to be served. The idea quickly spread. By 1889, cress sandwiches, muffins, cakes, crumpets and toasting forks were all very much in evidence.

The climax of the tea scene was the *thé dansant* (tea dance) of the early twentieth century – where mid-afternoon cream cakes were not the only temptation . . .

Sadly, regular afternoon tea parties died along with the lady of leisure during the Second World War, to be replaced by the dreaded machine brew which is so much a part of office life.

However, there are still opportunities for glorious old-fashioned tea parties: Sunday afternoons, family birthdays and christenings, to name a few. In fact the best tea parties are small gatherings on a winter afternoon, where the food is freshly baked and the table or trolley set with your best lace tablecloth and fine bone china; the fire burning brightly and the curtains drawn to exclude the wind and the rain.

Eight to ten guests is about the right number to ensure an interesting mix. Invite them by phone about a week ahead.

Plan to prepare the food as far as possible in advance. Scones and sponges are best made in the morning, but fruitcakes and tea-breads can safely be baked several days ahead and stored in airtight tins. Make the cakes, pastries and biscuits decorative and delicate to complement the flavour of the tea. Individual cakes and biscuits are best kept small (two- to three-bite-sized). Exotic cream confections are also good to offer at a tea party for small numbers. Remember to provide small pastry forks for your guests to eat with.

Victorian children were obliged to eat bread and butter before tackling the cake, and today many people prefer savoury sandwiches to the sweeter fare. Successful sandwiches are those which contain a delicious, moist filling, yet are small and elegant. A tea-time sandwich should be made with very thinly sliced bread, with the crusts removed. If you can't slice bread thinly – few of us are able to tackle the job with any degree of skill – buy the thin, ready-sliced variety. Avoid fillings which are too damp and butter each slice of bread thoroughly to protect it from the filling. Brown bread is the more popular and also stands up to 'wet' fillings better than white bread. Most sandwiches can be made in advance and kept fresh for five or six hours if sealed with clingwrap.

The tea however must be freshly made and should have been chosen with care. Teas with a high tannin content, such as Assam or Ceylon, are best kept for breakfast. For tea parties, use the more subtly flavoured teas, such as Lapsang Souchong, or try one of the new fruit-flavoured teas (mango tea is delicious). The advantage of the more delicate teas is that they can be left to brew for longer without spoiling. They also go further because you can simply top up the pot with boiling water.

Tea should be made in a china or glazed earthenware teapot which has been previously warmed. Allow one teaspoon of tea per person and use only freshly drawn boiling water.

Despite much discussion on the subject, there really is no 'correct' sequence for adding milk to tea. However, cold milk added first does protect fine bone china cups from the hot tea. Sugar should always be offered separately. Serve green tea without any addition. For China tea offer a thin slice of lemon. Indian tea can be taken with sugar, lemon, milk or mint.

Americans love iced tea. Make it by straining freshly made, not too strong, hot Indian tea into a heatproof jug, adding a little sugar and a squeeze of orange, lime or lemon juice, then stirring until the sugar dissolves; cool, cover and chill for about three hours. Serve in tall glasses with chunks of ice.

BARBECUES
Holding an impromptu barbecue party can be great fun. The secret of success is simple food for small numbers, coupled with realistic contingency plans to cope with any change in the weather.

A barbecue not only brings out long-forgotten food

flavours (somehow food always tastes better outdoors), it also provides an opportunity for guests to join in the preparation of the meal. Everyone will want to help.

Barbecue parties also offer a unique atmosphere of informality ideally suited to entertaining people of mixed age groups, including children over seven.

You don't need a lorry-load of expensive equipment, just a charcoal fire and a grill. If you have a back garden, it's quite easy to improvise a barbecue with a couple of bricks and some expanding wire. If, on the other hand, you have a balcony, it might be better to invest in a portable, commercially produced barbecue. Both with a bit of care should produce equally good results. The only crucial factor is the distance between the top of the charcoal and the grill. This should be adjustable from about 2 inches (5 cm) for fast searing to 4½ inches (12 cm) for slow cooking.

The other important point about a barbecue party is to remember to light the fire in good time. Cooking can only begin when the charcoal begins to show a surface of grey or white ash.

Small modern barbecues produce a surprisingly large amount of cooked food. The smallest portable barbecue cooks enough meat for four guests at any one time and a grill of about 12 × 20 inches (30 × 50 cm) is adequate for a party of eight. Limit your guests to twenty, be prepared to start cooking the food in good time and serve in relays.

Shop with care and expect to spend rather more than usual. Besides the need to offer a wide selection of meats, shopping for a barbecue involves striking the right balance between time and money to suit your circumstances. For optimum speed and little or no work, go to the best local food retailer and choose specially prepared kebabs, packs of chicken drumsticks, small chops, etc. Pick the freshest fruit and vegetables you can find.

Plan to prepare the food as far as possible in advance. Marinate the meats and, if necessary, make up the kebabs the night before. Prepare the salads and sauces, and partially bake the potatoes, in the microwave if you have one, on the morning of the party. Dress the salads only at the last moment. Likewise bake the rolls and any French bread just before the guests arrive. That way they can appreciate the tempting smell of your fresh 'home' baking.

Delicious dips help keep hunger pangs at bay while the meat is cooking. Make up two: one with garlic, one less pungent, and provide plenty of fresh crudités and crisps for dipping.

For the main course, cook marinated meat (chops, chicken and kebabs) in batches and serve trayloads at a time for guests to help themselves. Provide plenty of different salads and some interesting sauces to go with the meat.

Strictly speaking, a pudding or dessert is an unnecessary extra at a barbecue. Bananas baked in their skins on top of the grill are fun to offer, though, or you could offer ice cream, a big French fruit tart, or any fresh-cream confection you find at the patisserie.

On the drinks side, you could welcome guests with Pimm's, the perfect summer drink, and serve good red and white wine with the food. Offer children apple punch, garnished with slices of apple, or cans of Coke.

To set the scene, long trestle tables hired from your local DIY store are ideal for a barbecue. For a children's party, use brightly-coloured disposable plates, cups, glasses and paper napkins to avoid breakages, cut lips and fingers (not to mention the washing-up). For adults, use pretty earthenware crockery, stainless steel cutlery and checked tablecloths with matching napkins.

Hold the party near a power point and a suitable retreat (a large garage, verandah or barn) in case the heavens open. Alternatively put up a large tarpaulin extending from one side of your house.

Position the barbecue between the tables where you plan to eat and the table bearing the uncooked food.

For an evening party, good lighting is important. Guests need to be aware of ponds, swings, sandpits and other possibly dangerous obstacles in the garden. The cook must also be able to see what he or she is cooking. If possible use a couple of floodlights to show off your house and garden. Fairy lights can be strung from trees.

Flies and other insects can be a pest at certain times of the year. Keep them away from your food and your guests with a special white electric lamp. Insect-repellent torches and candles offer a practical, pretty and cheaper way to keep the May bugs at bay. You will find all three types of insect repellent at your local department store.

Music is a must for almost any party. For a small, informal barbecue, good, up-to-date tapes and some reliable hi-fi equipment should be sufficient. But if you plan to have music that is audible outside, for heaven's sake warn the neighbours.

Dress can of course be casual. Jeans and T-shirts are ideal and, if you're a guest, take a sweater – the evening will probably turn chilly later on. Above all, don't worry too much about throwing a barbecue: it's not a grand occasion.

KITCHEN SUPPERS

In the past, supper was what people gave their children before pushing them off to bed and out of the way. But today supper can be a marvellously relaxed and civilized way to entertain friends within the confines of a tight budget.

What supper *must* be is simple. So invite just a few friends by phone a few days in advance. Tell them to come in casual clothes and suggest a time to suit your own lifestyle.

Plan a menu to provide stylish, inexpensive food but avoid anything really cheap, such as offal, which is better reserved for wholesome everyday meals, where the complication of guests' likes and dislikes can be avoided.

Atmosphere matters even more when there are just a few of you. A warm kitchen smelling of good things provides the right setting. Lay the table with everyday knives and forks, plain wine glasses and a simple jug of small flowers in the centre. Try to be tidy as you prepare the meal. Minor emergencies can occur in the best-regulated households and set your schedule awry; worse still, your guests might arrive early. Preparing supper is one occasion when you must wash up as you work: your kitchen will be on show all evening. Cooking clutter stacked on the draining board does not suggest a relaxed approach to life; it just looks ugly.

To avoid making too much of a mess in the first place, plan the food with care. Restrict items to those requiring the minimum of serving dishes and little or no last-minute attention. Forget about puddings altogether: offer just two courses, a simple starter and a robust main course followed by some good cheese.

Drinks before the meal are always a welcome ice-breaker. Offer whatever you like – you know your friends' drinking habits best. During supper serve plenty of wine and mineral water.

Finish with good coffee and chocolates.

Other things which help to make a supper party swing are:

- a warm house: few people enjoy a meal at sub-zero temperatures; in the spring, especially, bright sunny days change quickly into chilly nights;
- music: if your tapes are useless ask your friends to bring a selection; don't forget to give them back when they leave;
- after-supper entertainment: ask musical friends to bring along their instruments; or have one of the new board games or cards available; during winter it is fun to have a jigsaw in progress, too;
- lighting: subdued lighting helps disguise any tattiness in the décor or furniture and makes for an intimate atmosphere, so switch off the kitchen strip light or spots; use soft combination lighting instead – small side lamps on the dresser or work surfaces and candles in brass or glass holders for the table.

AFTER-THEATRE PARTIES

Entertaining friends at home after the theatre can be fun but needs to be an organized procedure rather than an *ad hoc* invitation. By the time you get home, the chances are that everyone will be tired and hungry. You may not feel like cooking and your guests will certainly not want to sit around sipping yet more drinks and waiting for their food.

After-theatre suppers must be planned and most of the work completed before you leave for the theatre. Here's a checklist:
- lay the table;

- put out the wine and stow the mineral water in the fridge;
- wash and prepare the salads;
- make the salad dressing;
- prepare your chosen dish and leave it to cook in a low oven;
- make the pudding;
- have a tray ready for coffee.

When you plan the menu remember that rich, heavy meals are not conducive to a good night's sleep. Forget about a starter – hungry people usually prefer to tuck into their main course straight away. Make the main dish a light chicken, fish or vegetable bake. Serve with a couple of interesting salads. Offer something delicious, light and fruity for pudding. Finish with decaffeinated coffee and mint chocolates.

WEEKEND PARTIES

Having guests to stay for the weekend can be a relaxed, refreshing interlude or a nail-biting ordeal. Which it is depends to a large extent upon the occasion and your choice of guests. Close friends and family, who are presumably attuned to your lifestyle, should present few problems (apart from the odd family row: few of us can play Happy Families indefinitely). On the other hand, complete or comparative strangers, who may expect you to live up to a certain kind of lifestyle, may prove more difficult.

A country house party today differs greatly from those reconstructed for television. A good guest knows that in private homes the kids must be fed, the animals exercised, the phone answered and the office reading done, as well as cooking the food and dancing the night away. Indeed, most guests are enjoying a brief break from performing the same juggling act themselves.

The moral for a house-party hostess is to pick guests who will fit in with her way of life and forget to invite the rest.

Plan a weekend in the same way as you would a dinner party. The principle is the same: the difference is that the preparation needs to be on a larger scale, and takes longer.

Here are some of the points to remember.

Buy or order extra milk and make sure you have a stock of muesli and at least one other type of breakfast cereal. Breakfast rolls and hot croissants are more interesting and less work than endless rounds of toast. Provide plenty of butter, salted and unsalted, as well as low-fat spread.

Freshly-squeezed orange juice is heaven for two people but too time-consuming for a crowd. Instead buy large cartons of the best fresh orange juice from your supermarket.

Buy a stock of vacuum-packed ground coffee or grind fresh beans in advance and store in a screw-top jar in the fridge.

Plan a menu for every meal you intend to prepare and stick it on your kitchen wall as a reminder in moments of crisis.

Check household supplies. See that there is plenty of loo paper *in the loo* (it's no good hidden away in the store cupboard), tissues in the bedrooms, soap by the basins and a brush or plastic scourer with which to clean the bath by the bath.

Make sure you have plenty of clean bed linen. You need a bottom sheet, two pillowcases, a duvet cover and two towels for each single guest, plus a duvet. Check your store of pillows: ours goes down at an alarming rate. For large gatherings most young guests will bring sleeping bags if asked.

A guest's bedroom should be:

(1) warm: provide an electric fan-heater if possible; background heating may be inadequate for some;
(2) welcoming: flowers on the dressing-table, current magazines by the bed, a glass for water and a hot-water bottle or electric blanket.
(3) comfortable: it's hard to be good company next day if you've spent the night in a lumpy bed.

Other comforts to provide include hangers, sewing kit, bubble bath, shampoo, shower cap and aspirin.

Their basic needs satisfied, guests will expect a certain amount of food and entertainment throughout their stay. The best arrangements combine the two. Try to time the visit to coincide with some specific event such as the local hunt ball or race meeting; or make Saturday dinner at a local restaurant the main event (this provides you with an excuse to escape from the kitchen and gives your guests an opportunity to dress up and see a bit of local life).

In practice most weekends follow much the same pattern; only the size and scale of the entertainments will vary according to your means and your guests' tastes.

The secret of success lies in making your plans sufficiently flexible to allow for a sudden change in the weather, while recognizing that most guests prefer an organized programme rather than hanging about aimlessly for hours.

House guests often feel rather shy and awkward, particularly on their first morning, so concentrate on making them feel at ease. They will feel more relaxed if they know what to expect in advance: people in unfamiliar circumstances are easily flustered and bringing the wrong clothes or not knowing the form can spoil a potentially good day. So if you plan a fishing trip, warn them. That way they can either bring their waders or find a long-lost cousin in the district to visit.

In addition remember to warn all guests about plumbing peculiarities or activated burglar alarm systems: for example, if using the downstairs loo after midnight causes the alarm to wake the neighbourhood and the plug to be pulled on next door's swimming pool (this actually happened once, according to the reminiscences of a famous actor).

Finally, for heaven's sake *say* when you want to go to bed. Likewise indicate clearly what time you propose to serve breakfast, or whether your guests are free to sleep on.

A weekend timetable

Friday Ask guests to arrive about 7 p.m., in time for a drink before changing. Supper at 8.45 p.m., or on to the dance.

Saturday This should be a day to relax and enjoy fresh country air. Breakfast is a treat at the weekend for most busy people. Make yours special with oven-baked sausages wrapped round with bacon, hot croissants and ground coffee.

After such a feast the good guest disappears for a while. Saturday morning for the hostess is likely to be frantically busy. By mid-morning, most of the daily chores will be completed. This is the time for any self-respecting hostess to arrange an expedition – almost anywhere will do – followed by a light lunch (possibly a picnic at some sporting event).

Saturday dinner is usually considered the main event of the day. If you plan a dinner party, make it black tie. People love a chance to dress up. Serve drinks from 7 p.m. onwards. Ask a few locals to join you to add a bit of sparkle and a few fresh faces. Alternatively make up a party and go to a restaurant. When the locals depart, offer your guests a nightcap and resist the temptation to conduct a post mortem before you all troop off to bed.

Sunday Studying the Sunday papers helps both family and guests to fill the yawning gap after breakfast, while the cook (probably you) bustles about in the kitchen. The faithful may opt for church (keep a list of service times for the main denominations on your kitchen noticeboard). Serve drinks from noon onwards, followed by lunch, after which, with luck, your guests will go home and you can put your feet up.

CHAPTER 5

Picnic parties

There are two types of picnic: the highly organized type and the impromptu decision to pack up food for lunch and take it to the beach, river or park. The pleasure of eating outside is the same. This chapter focuses on the organized picnic, which demands a clear head and some careful planning in order to arrive at the chosen picnic spot with the food intact and nothing missing.

Organized picnic parties themselves fall into two distinct categories: elegant summer occasions – at the races, a regatta, or any sophisticated outdoor event – on the one hand; and on the other, more informal sporting picnics, often in chilly weather, where the food at least is warm and comforting.

In either case, planning to entertain far from home needs plenty of thought. Besides supplying the food, the host must, in many cases, be responsible for arranging admission to the event. He or she must therefore tread carefully to ensure that guests know the form: not only the written rules about dress but the unwritten ones set to trip the socially unaware.

ELEGANT SUMMER PICNICS
When organizing a party for the more sophisticated sporting events of the season, the state of your finances and the various entry requirements will probably dictate numbers. As a rule, six adults is about the maximum number you can comfortably cater for, unless you have plenty of money to spend on hired help and extra transport.

For a picnic party you need a table and some chairs. Many people are happy to stand about sipping drinks and nibbling smoked salmon canapés for a while, but most sink gratefully into a seat to tackle their main course, given the opportunity. In any case, you need a table to set out the food: rummaging about in the boot of the car ruins both hats and hair.

Flowers, a pretty cloth and matching napkins all help to make a picnic table look special. If you plan to picnic frequently it's worth investing in proper melamine picnic ware. Look for the 'dishwasher-proof' sign. Large department stores usually have an excellent selection in the spring. They also stock a large range of stylish picnic hampers and baskets. Buy a plain hamper or basket and avoid wasting your hard-earned money on the various fitted-out varieties, which cost a fortune. Then work out your plate and container requirements and buy accordingly, but take knives, forks and spoons from home.

The cold box or bag, used to transport food and keep wine fresh, has completely revolutionized modern picnics. Invest in at least one. If you have very thirsty friends and a large car, invest in the best: a huge, almost trunk-sized cool box which takes twelve bottles.

Champagne tastes better in inexpensive glasses rather than plastic beakers. Always pack glasses individually in kitchen-paper towels.

Whatever equipment you choose, remember to pack everything carefully away out of sight when you leave the car and *lock* the boot.

Other practical items useful for picnics include a couple of tea-towels, a sponge or cloth, plastic bags for the dirty cutlery and plates and a black plastic bag for the rubbish.

Food for an elegant picnic must be special, yet portable and not too messy. Aim for a simple menu using the best ingredients. Here are some suggestions.

Starters:
pâté, made with smoked fish or meats;
savoury profiteroles;
savoury roulade;
handsome slices of Scotch smoked salmon (put on plates at
    home and sealed with clingwrap for easy service) with
    lemon wedges.

Main course:
foil-wrapped cold fillet of beef (carved on the spot); or cold poached salmon;
two or three interesting salads in sealed containers;
french dressing in a screw-top jar.

Dessert:
strawberries, hulled at home, with thick cream and meringues (remember to include a jar of castor sugar).

Coffee is best made on the spot. Use instant with water from a vacuum flask filled with boiling water. Don't forget to pack a few teaspoons.

Owing to the vagaries of the weather, summer events in real life rarely bear much resemblance to glossy magazine pictures. That being said, most people going to one of these events want to look their best.

The general rule is to wear your best clothes but steer clear of high-heeled shoes, which will be ruined and are in any case not practical for walking across potentially muddy fields.

INFORMAL SPORTING PICNICS
Informal sporting events can provide an excellent opportunity for entertaining family and friends in a relaxed atmosphere. Plenty of fresh air and generous supplies of hearty food are the order of the day.

Polo and point-to-point
Polo begins in April and lasts throughout the summer. Not only does it offer a healthy day out in the open air for a fraction of the cost of most other sporting events, polo also provides an opportunity for ordinary folk to indulge in that other well-known, less strenuous sport of spotting the royals.

As weekend polo matches do not begin until mid-afternoon, spectators have ample time to arrive at their chosen club and enjoy a picnic lunch beforehand. The best way to eat at a polo match is from a hamper stowed in the boot of a car. Here are some suggestions for its contents on a chilly spring day:

hot, thick stew from a wide-necked vacuum flask;
warm baked potatoes wrapped in foil;
warm herb bread, foil-wrapped and packed in a wide-necked vacuum flask;
scotch eggs;
slices of quiche;
salads;
a large joint of ham or beef, to be carved on the spot.

To drink, take good medium sherry, very welcome in cold weather and recommended by ancient polo devotees, who claim it goes 'straight to their toes'. Whisky mixed with ginger wine to make Whisky Mac is also good for keeping out the cold, while chilled champagne warms the soul whatever the weather.

The best polo parties feature cars and Land Rovers overflowing with people, picnic hampers, muddy boots and extra shoes. They tend to be multi-family occasions on a 'bring-your-own-food' basis (naturally each car-load also brings plenty of booze to offer friends). It's great fun to be the instigator of the outing, to become a sort of 'team leader', so aim to organize a group of friends, complete with offspring, to join you in convoy. A fleet of cars drawn up on the side of the pitch forms a perfect base for this sort of party. The expense of the drink is shared: there's a well-stocked bar in every boot (don't forget the soft drinks for the drivers). The food is often shared too, as everyone tends to over-cater. Meanwhile you get all the credit for arranging the afternoon.

Dress for polo varies. For example, at Windsor the safest wear for men is a blazer and flannels, with a smart shirt and silk tie. Cirencester and Cowdray are less formal and more tweedy. For women almost anything goes, including trousers.

In any event, make sure you and your party wear shoes or wellies suitable for 'treading in'. This is a quaint custom which helps keep the ground in good condition and provides spectators with the opportunity to get their circulation going again, as they all troop out on to the pitch at half-time and between games to stamp back into place the divots of churned-up turf.

There are about twenty polo clubs scattered over the United Kingdom. The most popular, and the places where one is most likely to see and be seen, are the four main clubs in the south of England: Cirencester Park, Cowdray Park, the Guards (at Windsor) and Ham.

All clubs make a small charge for cars and their occupants. For this you are entitled to park directly on the sidelines of the pitch: members on one side, the public on the other.

The uninitiated may like to know that the tatty tin or wooden huts on the members' side of the pitch are called club pavilions, while the white or striped tents crowded with smart middle-aged ladies and gentlemen sipping champagne are the domain of the commercial sponsors and their guests.

Picnics at horse trials or local point-to-point meetings follow much the same pattern as those described for polo. Wear warm country gear and offer hot, comforting food and plenty to drink. Again, try to go in a crowd: nothing is worse than loitering in small groups at these affairs. On a seasonal note, add game pie to the hamper, and be prepared to eat in the car if it rains, remembering to choose foods which are easy to eat and serve, and not too messy.

Shooting lunches

When planning a shooting lunch, the most important thing to remember is that the guests will almost certainly be both cold and hungry.

Where to hold your lunch depends upon custom and your accommodation. Some of the best shooting lunches take place in barns or other similarly draughty farm buildings set with trestle tables. If this is the case, there's not much anyone can do about the surroundings. A checked tablecloth with matching napkins and large, handsome earthenware plates rather than bone china and inexpensive glass are the order of the day. Otherwise the warmth of your welcome must express itself in a good supply of hot food and decent wine.

The geniality of your guests is almost certainly assured, since drinking is an integral part of shooting. Generally the guns (those taking part in the shooting) are offered a 'pipe opener' on arrival: a bottle to pass round while pegs are drawn for who shoots where and when. Two or occasionally three drives are made before lunch, each interspersed with celebratory drinks, occasionally home-made cherry brandy or sloe gin in small silver cups. Naturally the people who arrive with the lunch are very welcome indeed.

Hearty, hot and filling food is the most acceptable. So serve thick, tasty stews full of meat and vegetables, plenty of potatoes, mashed or baked, and one or two relishes. Follow on with stilton, apples and chunks of freshly baked wholemeal bread. Finish with fruit cake.

Naturally you will also offer wine with the above meal. Offer a good, full-bodied red, plus some reasonable port and perhaps hot strong coffee to finish.

Don't be surprised if lunch is taken at speed. The guns are usually eager to catch the rest of the light.

If you're taking part in the shooting, it's a good idea to take a spare pair of shoes and a sports jacket in the boot of your car in case lunch is served in the house.

CHAPTER 6

Family occasions

This chapter contains advice for special family celebrations – plans to help you organize those once-in-a-lifetime occasions like weddings or christening parties, plus a few fresh ideas to help you cope with the more informal gatherings such as Christmas.

It goes without saying that attempting to organize any family event takes a degree of tact and skill. The secret of success lies in frequent consultation and a sense of humour. That is not to suggest you need heed all the advice so generously proffered; indeed you may prefer to forget the greater part immediately. What you must remember is to use charm and a sweet smile to soften the impact of any potentially controversial decisions.

The three golden rules for coping with any family party are:

(1) outline your objectives;
(2) establish your priorities;
(3) keep a sense of proportion.

To this might be added: smile... even when it hurts.
Have fun.

WEDDING PARTIES

Weddings are traditionally family occasions. When it comes to arranging a daughter's marriage, most parents are anxious to 'do their best' and that's where the dilemma starts: how to put on a wedding party that is lavish but not extravagant, elegant without being ostentatious.

Here's a checklist to help you plan assuming a full-scale church wedding and smart reception.

☐ Guest list (both bride and groom)
☐ Budget
☐ Invitations
☐ Bride's dress
☐ Bridesmaids' dresses
☐ Bride's bouquet
☐ Bridesmaids' bouquets
☐ Church
☐ Service sheets
☐ Choir
☐ Organist
☐ Bells
☐ Carpet
☐ Cleaners
☐ Flowers (church and reception)
☐ Venue (or marquee hire)
☐ Caterers (cake, party food)
☐ Drink
☐ Toastmaster
☐ Photographer
☐ Speeches (who to give?)
☐ Transport (to/from church, to/from reception)

One glance at the above list is surely enough to convince you that rule number one must be: keep a cool head.

Whether you're a traditional Mum or Dad or an ultra-modern parent, it pays to remember that you are dealing with two families whose lifestyles may be completely different and whose individual hopes and aspirations may not necessarily coincide. Relationships may therefore be strained; personalities may clash; offence may be taken where none is intended. A thoughtful approach and careful planning can overcome many of these difficulties. However, some minor upsets are inevitable, no matter how carefully you tread. If that is the case, just try to relax and remember that over-dramatization just makes matters worse.

Numbers

As for most parties, wedding plans begin with the guest list. (Some end there, too.) Make a start with everyone you would like to invite and, if you're family-minded, everyone you ought to ask. Include dreary old Aunt Maud and dotty cousin Jasper as well as all your fascinating friends at this stage. The list will be huge. No matter: this way you will gain some idea of the numbers involved and make sure no one is left out.

Next, prune away long-lost relations living abroad: they may like to receive an invitation but they are most unlikely to come; likewise Great Aunt Norah in the nursing home, but she too will be pleased to have been invited.

Once the list looks less daunting, review the financial situation. Perhaps discuss the possibility of sharing expenses with the bridegroom or his parents. Whether your concern is about cash, or a surplus of dreary cousins, there is usually some room for compromise.

If you're a strict traditionalist and pushed for funds, why not consider the advantages of an intimate family wedding? The bride and groom can always celebrate with their friends at a later date.

On the other hand, if you're financially secure but feel one or other family is too dull to bear, you could choose to hold a dance or disco for young friends following the formal reception. Only consider this if you can afford it. There's no point in holding a very large, very grand wedding, complete with a ball in the evening, if you cannot provide an equally lavish quantity of food and drink.

In some cases the size of the church will automatically determine the number of guests you can invite to the service. Should this be a problem, the answer is to have two separate invitations printed for the day's events: invitations for the church and reception, and invitations for the reception only.

Invitations

For advice on having invitations printed, see page 17. Below is the normally accepted form of wording for a wedding invitation:

Mr and Mrs Steven Smith
request the pleasure of
the company of

....

at the marriage of their daughter
Belinda
to
Jason Wilson
at St Mary's Church, Oxted
on Saturday 8th June 1988
at 2.30 p.m.
and afterwards at The Moat House

RSVP   Morning Dress
The Moat House
Barrow Green
Oxted
Surrey

Here is a suggested form of wording for those who plan to arrange their own wedding:

Isobel French and Clive Hanson

request the pleasure of the company of

....

at St Mary's Church, Chelsea

on Thursday 5th November at 4 p.m.

and afterwards

at Claridge's, Brook Street, London W1

RSVP
16 Marlborough Road
London N1

Wedding gear

At very smart weddings the men don the everyday dress of our Victorian ancestors, while the women slip into something new and expensive bought specially for the occasion.

Many men look very good in morning dress. This means a black or grey tailcoat and top hat, worn with an appropriate waistcoat and trousers (dove-grey waistcoat and striped trousers with a black coat; matching fabric waistcoat and trousers with a grey coat).

The complete morning dress uniform can be hired if necessary. Dinner-jackets and tailcoats are often passed down from father to son, seemingly immune to the whims of fashion.

However, not all weddings are formal today. If you want to save your guests embarrassment, state your preference on the invitation: morning dress, morning dress optional, or suits. (Sadly, we have no stylish wording for suits: the French *tenue de ville* sounds much smarter, but isn't in general use.)

What to wear at weddings in other parts of the world

presents more of a problem. If in any doubt, ring up and find out. The price of an intercontinental call will be worth every penny for peace of mind. Don't forget that formal wear can always be hired in major cities all over the world – you don't have to cart your clobber halfway round the globe.

The ceremony

A country church wedding in summer is still considered by some to be the most romantic. For a second marriage, however, a full church wedding may not be possible. If one partner has been divorced, a registry office ceremony is the only alternative. Church of England vicars will often follow a civil wedding with a church blessing, but Roman Catholics are presently offered no such official recognition.

If the wedding is to be held in church, a rehearsal is essential, whatever the ceremony or the size and scale of the wedding, to ensure that everyone knows exactly what they are expected to do on the day. Hold the rehearsal as late as possible, preferably on the previous afternoon.

Experts assure me that a thorough rehearsal helps calm pre-wedding nerves, so include bridesmaids and pages in your plans, if possible. It's a good idea for the bride to wear a long skirt and, if the wedding dress has a long train, pin a large sheet to her shoulders so that the young attendants know what to expect. An organized practice, that is, walking the length of the church in a long dress and getting used to handling and manoeuvring a train, should make for a smooth trip up the aisle on the day.

Organ, choir and good music add a sense of occasion to the wedding ceremony. In addition, beautiful music eases tension and keeps the congregation happy should any delay occur. Count the extra cost involved as money well spent.

Have one adult person in charge of the bridesmaids and pages. The best man and the chief bridesmaid are always too busy to cope. Arrange hassocks or footstools in the aisle for small attendants to sit on during the service, and seat their parents near the front of the church. Children feel more secure if they can see their Mum and Dad. Jelly beans judiciously handed out by the adult-in-charge will also help keep the very young happy. Find out where the loo is (if there is one) and remember to tell the adult-in-charge.

After the service
After the religious service the register has to be signed. However, the event does not need to be witnessed by Uncle Tom Cobbleigh and all – most vestries are too small to accommodate a crowd. Parents, grandparents, the eldest brother or sister and the best man can bring the total to over fourteen, more than enough to manoeuvre in and out of a small space. So keep the numbers down, the signing speedy and suggest that the rest of the family remain seated to enjoy the music.

Hanging about outside the church on a windy day waiting for the photographs to be taken is no fun for anyone. A much better idea is for the bride to progress down the aisle, pause briefly at the porch door, and proceed to her waiting car or carriage. A good professional photographer will get perfect (and far more natural) pictures under these conditions and the guests will avoid an attack of pneumonia.

The formal portraits of the bride and the two families are best taken immediately upon arrival at the reception, before the guests are received. Most professionals are quite familiar with this procedure.

Under no circumstances ask a friendly guest to take the photographs even if he or she is a professional photographer. The results will almost certainly be disappointing, if indeed they ever reach you.

Flowers
Good flowers are wonderful. But you do need a lot of them to make any impact at a wedding, so budget accordingly. Some churches have tied arrangements with specific florists, as do many of the big hotels. This may or may not be good news. At my wedding the guests enjoyed not just our flowers, but also two splendid arrangements on the high altar that had been ordered for the preceding ceremony.

Flowers for country weddings offer more scope. You may have a couple of friends who are particularly good at decorating the local church. Alternatively the nearest flower-arranging ladies' guild may be pleased to help. Best of all are the people who 'do flowers' for parties, weddings, etc. (see list on pages 115-16). They are the real professionals, who buy at the central markets and can be relied upon not to produce stiff gladioli pedestals as your local florist might. They have an excellent eye for colour and, even more important, they will design a flower scheme just for you. As always when dealing with professionals, ask to see a written estimate before you place an order.

Transport
Smooth, reliable, well-organized transport is crucial for a wedding party and is best left to the professionals. Talk to a couple of car-hire companies, get a written estimate and ask to see their cars before you make a booking. Always ask for a written confirmation of any such booking.

If you plan a wedding at a large hotel and are using the planning facilities offered by the banqueting department, special arrangements will be included for wedding cars. This will leave you free to fret about something else. However, some hotel receptionists have been known to hand over unnecessarily large tips to the drivers, which are naturally added to your bill. So beware: check the cost, plus the service charge, and ask about the drivers' gratuities before you give the green light.

Timing is all-important at weddings. A bride is always allowed to be a few minutes late. But that is all: delays of more than twenty minutes are discourteous to the guests and alarming for the groom. When you arrange the transport, discuss with your chosen car-hire company the time allowed for each journey, the traffic conditions and any parking restrictions. In addition ask for a written timetable to accompany the estimate, so that you both know the exact programme. Remember to send a copy of the transport arrangements to the bridegroom's parents.

The reception
When it comes to planning a wedding reception, my advice is to keep it short. If you invite more than 50 people it's a good idea to engage a professional major-domo or toast-master to keep the proceedings on course. A wedding

reception marks the end of a particularly busy and hectic period for everyone involved, yet distant relations and friends from afar long to talk. A firm hand is needed to move events forward without causing hurt feelings. The professional major-domo in his dashing red coat can control the situation and keep things moving without seeming bossy or rude.

If you are planning a formal wedding, consider carefully whether you wish to have a receiving line: it can cause a long delay if both sets of parents, the best man, the bridesmaids and the pages all line up. On the other hand, a receiving line not only allows the principal participants to greet their guests, but also provides the guests with an opportunity to meet, often for the first time, their host and hostess. Many guests feel acutely uncomfortable in situations where they are unable to recognize them; even worse should they be obliged to introduce themselves.

Modern wedding planners suggest the proceedings may be speeded up if only the bride and groom greet their guests. This system has the advantage of allowing the parents and other principal participants more time to circulate within the party, chat a fraction longer to old friends and generally make guests feel welcome. It does not however overcome the problem of instant recognition – unless you follow commercial cocktail party practice and give the home team labels to wear!

Country weddings held in the morning are still sometimes followed by a formal seated luncheon, the original wedding breakfast. It is a lovely idea: greeting guests with a glass of champagne in idyllic surroundings, then hosting an appetizing meal eaten at leisure and in comfort. But this type of reception does take a very long time: the receiving line, the meal, the cake-cutting ceremony, not to mention the speeches; and the host must also be prepared to spend a great deal of money, not to mention time and effort. This explains why an afternoon wedding is more usual now, followed by a modest buffet reception.

Quite apart from the amount of money saved, the provision of food for an afternoon wedding reception presents few problems. Most people are not particularly hungry at four or five o'clock. A selection of light sweet and savoury items is all that is required: it is tea time, after all. That is not, however, to recommend the DIY approach – self-catering for a wedding party is a recipe for disaster. Relying on other members of the immediate family is equally unwise. Instead, ask a reliable caterer to provide a simple buffet. Insist that both tea and coffee are offered as well as champagne. (Many elderly relatives will be reluctant to drink more than one small glass of alcohol and drivers, too, will be grateful for a cup of tea.)

When ordering drinks for a reception, champagne is the natural choice, but it is expensive. However there are other acceptable alternatives (see suggestions on page 27).

The real trouble with drinks at weddings is that people seem particularly thirsty on such occasions. Hence time is money: funding an adequate supply of wine to serve friends and family for one-and-a-half to two hours is one thing; allowing the party to drag on for three hours or more not only doubles the bill, it drives bored guests to drink – another good reason for fixing a programme in advance and allowing the major-domo a free hand to move the proceedings along.

Cutting the wedding cake is a signal for speeches at the reception. You may like them or loathe them, but you must have at least one speech – a toast to the bride and groom – to provide a sense of occasion.

Almost more important than the number of speeches is the length. For my money a good speech is a short speech: nothing is worse than being forced to listen to a rambling monologue. Jokes can be equally irritating; jokes in bad taste alienate all but the least sensitive.

So select your speakers with care, and thank heaven for the virtual abolition of the telegram.

Whatever the quality of the speeches, they must be heard. A microphone may be a necessity: consider the acoustics of the hall or tent in advance and plan accordingly. Remember that small speakers evenly placed around the room provide a better distribution of sound than one or two huge ones. Some hotels have their own sound system. This is all very well, but on no account allow yourself to be lulled into a false sense of security. When you book the room, ask tactfully if you may test the system out. That way you can arrange for any necessary modification to be made. The work involved need not cost too much and the result will be well worth the extra cash involved. Even so, it is prudent to organize a rehearsal before the reception. Taps, whistles and squeaks are unnerving for the speaker and embarrassing for everyone else.

The speeches over, traditionally the major-domo collects the groom, presents the bride with her bouquet and escorts them away to change. It can be a sad moment for the bride: leaving all her friends behind just as she is beginning to relax and enjoy the party, not to mention taking off her unlikely-to-be-worn-again, brand-new wedding dress. This may be one reason why weddings have changed so much in recent years, with many brides staying on to the end of the reception. However, if the bride and groom are going away it's up to the best man to gather the guests together at the right moment to cheer and wish the departing couple good luck.

A tip for wedding planners from the doyenne party-planner herself: Lady Elizabeth Anson apparently slips a bottle of champagne and a box of canapés into the happy couple's luggage before they leave.

CHRISTENING PARTIES

A christening is essentially a private occasion. However, most proud parents like to follow the ceremony with some kind of celebration.

The type of hospitality you offer is, to some extent, dictated by the time of day. A morning ceremony provides an opportunity for a light buffet lunch or a drinks party. Which you choose depends upon your inclination and your purse: see Chapter 1 to help you plan either. An afternoon christening, on the other hand, calls for the more traditional christening tea: tiny sandwiches, small cakes, baby sausage rolls and savouries, and, of course, champagne and a christening cake.

Tradition also demands the reservation of the top tier of the wedding cake for the christening of the first child. The trouble is that even the best traditions can go stale with time. Certainly by the time my first child appeared, some eighteen months after the wedding, our cake was long past its best, with rock-hard, brittle icing, browning at the edges. My advice is to eat up your wedding cake and bake or buy a fresh one for the christening.

CHRISTMAS PARTIES

Parties at Christmas tend to be infectious. Just about everyone you meet has either definitely arranged to give one or is thinking about doing so. The trouble is, while most of us have a clear idea of our Christmas Day tradition, the various celebrations around it often become a blur, with very little to distinguish one from another.

Wrack your brains to think of a way to make your party different. A theme party is an excellent way to make your celebration stand out from the others, as long as you plan it carefully. See page 00 for suggestions for celebrations on a theme.

If you hate the idea of themes, offer a selection of foods as different as possible from roast turkey and mince pies.

Here's a suggested menu in which every item except the green vegetables can be frozen. Suitable recipes abound in any good cookery book.

Smoked salmon pin-wheel canapés with the drinks before-hand

Individual salmon or pink trout mousse
Warm wholemeal rolls and unsalted butter

Rich mixed game casserole, with port and redcurrant sauce

Fresh green broccoli and french beans

Chocolate roulade or caramelized oranges.

Whatever type of Christmas party you choose, start to plan early – October is almost too late – particularly if you intend to rely on hired help.

Check the provisional date with close friends in the area to make sure it doesn't clash with another party. If there is a clash, take a deep breath, telephone each guest and explain that you have to cancel the event. (There's no need to say exactly why.) But say you will be in touch at a later date. Once the date is settled, do send your invitations out in good time. People get booked up early around Christmas.

For family festivities, trying to be different is a waste of time. The anticipation and observation of a time-honoured tradition are part of the pleasure of Christmas at home. So go wild with red and green bows, have a huge Christmas tree, tie a holly wreath on the door, light open fires (or the gas look-alikes), bake mince pies and, if you have time, beat up your own brandy butter. But do not allow seasonal sentiments to impede practicality. Your sanity, your health and your bank balance all matter more than limitless Christmas comforts.

Decorations

Florist-trimmed holly wreaths bedecked with plastic roses and cellophane bows are hideously expensive. For more style and far less money, trim your own. Buy a plain green wreath from your local flower market and 3 yards (3 metres) of one-inch (2.5 cm) scarlet nylon ribbon. Fix a bow to the top of the wreath, wind the ribbon round each side to the base and tie long streamers to float in the wind. Secure the wreath with strong string on to your front door.

Unless you enjoy dashing about with dustpan and brush, be choosy about the type of Christmas tree you buy. The traditional variety sheds its needles in seconds. Instead buy the more reliable Scots pine, Noble fir or Caucasian fir, all available from good garden centres. Too many pine needles can clog even the most efficient vacuum cleaner. To avoid this situation, stand the tree in a container of water. Special metal adjustable tree stands are available, complete with pot. These must be topped up with water daily.

Very tall trees are difficult to acquire unless you grow your own. So if you want a big tree order early and arrange for delivery in about the second week in December, then keep it outside until required. Always spray your tree with a preserving aerosol spray before you bring it indoors.

Christmas cards are a happy reminder of friends near and far, but can be a menace if left to stand or fall down on surfaces and collect dust. Solve the problem by investing in a quantity of red ribbon and suspending the cards over the tops of mirrors, etc.

Beat the crowds and organize your Christmas table centrepiece in October when the shops are well stocked with interesting baubles. Buy red, silver and gold candles and any paperware too: the best are long gone by December.

Expensive crackers look magnificent on a Christmas table, the prizes inside are useful and the jokes passable. Cheap crackers are a complete waste of money: avoid them.

Food and drink
Make a menu plan of the meals for each day over the Christmas period. Choose as far as possible dishes that can be prepared in advance and frozen. That way you will be free to be with the family.

Stand-by soups and frozen baked potatoes take the hassle out of last-minute meals. For puddings, choose something light such as fruit sorbets or fruit mousses and make small, open mince tarts to reduce your pastry (and hence fat) intake. Brandy butter can be made weeks ahead and stored in the freezer. Excellent brandy butter can also be bought in good food stores. Extra brandy can be added on the day.

The best Christmas puddings and Christmas cake are always made at least three months ahead. Alternatively, buy both from your nearest high-quality food store.

Even a cook's memory can fail under pressure. To avoid last-minute panics, prepare a list of dishes in the freezer, together with the required defrosting times. Fix it on the front of the fridge door on Christmas Eve.

Remember to order and collect the Christmas drinks in good time, and always stock up with some non-alcoholic drinks for abstainers and drivers.

CHAPTER 7

Children's parties

One of the things most children look forward to is a birthday party. Most parents, on the other hand, are inclined to panic at the prospect of entertaining a crowd of other people's offspring. A noisy, disorganized children's party can be worse than a nightmare. On the other hand, a well run, thoroughly planned party can be not only a rewarding exercise for the young host/hostess (learning to give pleasure is all part of growing up) but great fun for both parent and child. Like most things in life success depends to a large extent upon the amount of time and effort you are willing to invest in the project.

For a start let me assure there is no *need* for children to create chaos to enjoy themselves. But they will if you let them.

The fact is that successful children's parties, like any other type of entertaining, do not happen by magic, but depend upon careful preparation and plenty of pre-planning. The good thing is that whatever the age of the child the technique is much the same. However, your child probably has little or no experience in the planning field therefore the bulk of the work must be undertaken by – guess who? You're dead right... you. That way everyone will have fun.

How many guests should you invite? Much depends upon your powers of persuasion. Some children are so socially minded they hope to invite the entire school, teaching staff, dinner ladies, groundsmen *et al*. Obviously you must gently dissuade them from such unbounded hospitality. Generally it is best to keep the numbers down, but to no less than six guests. (Specific suggestions are made under individual age groups later.) On every occasion set age limits and stick to them. Never invite older or younger brothers and sisters, as large age gaps spell disaster.

Under no circumstances invite your best friend's children or your godchildren, unless you know they get on well with your own. Small children and even some young adults are quite jealous of their parents' affection.

Always send written invitations to all age groups. Buy them or make them, but do send them through the post. Firstly, children love receiving them. More important, young children are often vague about names and where their friends live and the safe delivery of notes, message or anything else is rarely within their scope. (It's often beyond the scope of teenagers too, but that's another story.) It's also as well to recognize that many small children frequently forget who their friends *are*. So check the facts with the class teacher and let the Post Office arrange safe delivery. Remember to enclose a map for friends from far afield, and add your phone number, just in case they get lost.

For the venue, be realistic, be adventurous and remember that kids enjoy novelty.

If your living space is limited and your child insists on a large party, hire the village hall (or your local community centre) and hang the cost. Your sanity counts. (See pages 40-42 for other acceptable alternatives to a traditional party at home.)

On the other hand, if you have a large garden, why not plan a summer party? But beware the vagaries of the weather. Arrange simple alternative accommodation under cover, in case the heavens open. A tent, a garage or a barn will serve very well and preserve your precious paintwork and upholstery.

The real answer to accommodation problems for all age groups lies in positive thinking. Children expect to have fun. They don't especially care where. Décor is simply not important to them.

But there is something that should be very important to you. Unless you plan to spend the following few weeks on tranquillizers, you will need help in running a children's party. Trying to cope unaided is not just impossible, it is plain daft. Children of all ages are surprisingly receptive to atmosphere, and a tense, exhausted parent can quickly undermine the party spirit. Delegation is the name of the game.

A couple of friends can lend you moral support and provide sound practical help. Seek their advice at the planning stage. With luck, they'll offer to help. Talk through the party and agree areas where they may enjoy making a contribution. (Their enjoyment is crucial.) On the day, suggest they come early. Welcome them with a smile, even if you still have wet hair, and then leave them to their agreed tasks.

Have a small gift tucked away to give them after the party. A glass of wine is usually gratefully received too. You will all need a drink by then.

A successful children's party must include plenty of good food and plenty of good play. However, both the food and the play vary according to age. Basically there are four stages: under-threes, three-to-fives, five-to-nines, and ten-to-twelves.

UNDER-THREES
Children under three are not particularly social beings. They do not on the whole 'play' in the accepted sense. Co-operation with anyone, never mind their peer group, is not their strongest point and many in fact prefer adult company. Therefore, for the toddling 2-year-olds, bake a sponge cake, invite the grannies and grand-dads and perhaps one other special friend to tea, and save their first real party for later when they can enjoy it.

THREE-TO-FIVES
This age group loves the idea of a party. A parent's role is to make the reality live up to the idea.

Simplicity is the key to success: simple, informative invitations; simple, bright decorations; simple (not dull) food; and simple entertainment.

Restrict the numbers, no matter what. Five or six friends are enough for a 4-year-old; not more than a dozen for the rising fives. Invite only real friends. As a birthday approaches children often accumulate new friends at an alarming rate.

Gently suggest, if you dare, that mothers and fathers go home and leave their children to enjoy the party at their own pace. However, be prepared to be flexible. Some children are too fearful to allow their parents out of sight. If this is the case, *smile* and make them feel welcome. Remember, they would probably much prefer to go home and put their feet up for an hour.

Start early. Keep it short. Finish on time. Play it this way and everyone will have fun.

Basic party plan for the three-to-fives:

3.00 – 3.45 p.m. Arrival. Games.
3.45 – 4.30 p.m. Tea.
4.30 – 5.00 p.m. Free play, story time, entertainer, Father Christmas comes – what you will.
5.15 p.m. Home time (put it on the invitations).

Organize loo rounds on arrival, before tea and after tea.

Even if you're cramped for space try to keep the play area and the eating area separate. In any case always remove anything remotely precious. Likewise remove all keys from doors, particularly the bathroom and loo doors. Trailing lamp cords and unguarded electric sockets are other hazards to consider. Be sure all medicines are under lock and key, and place all chemical household cleaners out of reach and preferably out of sight.

Pretty paper plates and cups are a waste of money for this age group. For a start paper mugs tip over in a trice. Numbers are not a problem, so invest in good-quality re-usable bright picnicware instead. Never give a child a glass to drink from. Even the goody-goodies who remain seated wriggle about. A child on the move with glass to mouth is a terrifying sight.

Cover the table with a bright cloth but save the special effects for the next age group. Likewise forget crackers and balloons: some small children hate sudden noises.

Bear this in mind where games are concerned, and avoid loud, rough games. Chasing games too can terrify timid 3-year-olds at what may be their first party.

Break the ice with moving-about games such as hunt the slipper (or the ten-pence piece) while the children arrive.

Later introduce old-fashioned nursery favourites. Singing games help break down the shyness barrier: Farmer's in his Den (watch out they don't get too rough with the dog), Ring-a-ring-a-roses, Oranges and Lemons. Musical games are fun: Pass the Parcel, the Magic Mat, Musical Chairs.

Very young children get bored very quickly and their attention wanders, so have a long list of things to do to avoid awkward pauses. On the other hand do not be surprised if you receive requests to play the same game quite frequently, each time with equal success.

However, be warned. Other people's pre-school-age children can be quite unpredictable. Some hate all games. Some are just shy and need encouragement to join in. Others prefer to sit in the corner and play with the host's toys, often in quite a destructive fashion. Have a box of less precious toys ready in the corner to meet this eventuality and thus avoid your child's after-the-party tears.

For the food, you need small morsels arranged in several small dishes rather than large platters for this age group. Accordingly, provide lorry-loads of crisps and other snacks, small sausages, cheese biscuits, sandwiches, bridge rolls made to look like boats with cheese sails, fruit (satsumas are easy to peel), jelly in dishes (yes, it's still expected at parties for this age group) and as many jelly beans and other small sweets as your conscience allows. A quick trip to the local supermarket will provide almost all the food you need. Skip the traditional birthday fruitcake: children hardly ever get round to eating it. But they enjoy candles, so bake or buy a victoria sponge instead. Decorate it with some fondant icing and top with 'magic' candles (which light again unaided after being blown out), which you can buy from a confectioner or department store.

Do not fret if a child eats almost nothing at tea time. He or she may be particularly shy or just overawed by the occasion, but may creep back for a snack later. Full-up children like to cart their piece of cake home wrapped in a napkin to enjoy later.

FIVE-TO-NINES
It is important to run a party of this age group at a tremendous pace. If left unoccupied for any length

of time, the five-to-nines quickly become unholy terrors.

Again, write the invitations or, better still, get your offspring to write them. Provide clear details of the party programme, arrival time, fancy dress, etc. Choose the numbers to suit the age and character of your child.

Dressing up is fun for this age group. Little girls love it; boys enjoy it reluctantly, and most parents don't mind too much, as long as you choose an easy theme which involves minimal time and expenditure. Ideas for party themes include Twelfth Night (good for younger children who hate the idea of Christmas being over), Fairyland, Mad Hatter and company, Tramps, Pancakes, Cowboys and Indians, Pirates, Druids (at Midsummer), Cops and Robbers, Romans (dress: togas or tunics and breastplates), Fireworks (5 November), Witches and Wizards (Hallowe'en), Ghosts and Ghoulies, Space Invaders and Star Trek.

This age group is competitive by nature, so team games are tops. Rough rolling-on-the-floor games are just as popular... if you allow them. Undoubtedly this is the time when you will have the most fun. Even so you will need plenty of stamina, several helpers and a very long list of games to play.

There are some excellent games books available from good bookshops. Invest in one and adapt or alter games to suit your chosen theme.

If this information still leaves you feeling daunted at the prospect of organizing a party for your child, why not consider using an entertainer? The cost is not too prohibitive, particularly if by spending a little money you enjoy the party too. Entertainers will either take care of the entire proceedings or simply provide an hour's show. The choice is yours (see list on page 117).

The 'going home present' is still *de rigueur* – give it up at your peril. Your offspring will certainly suffer at school next day if you ignore the custom. No matter how much you spend on the party, if you fail to provide a token gift you will certainly be considered mean.

There are many acceptable alternatives to the traditional party at home. All require a packed lunch or tea and involve you in some expense, so why not get together with other parents to ease the cost, share the workload and make the day more fun for yourself?

You might hire an open-top bus complete with driver and conductor and do a city tour while the kids munch crisps and see the sights. Another idea is to hire a mini-bus and take a party of kids to a safari park.

If you live near water, hire a longboat or barge with bargeman and boat boy and, if you're lucky, a bar. Or organize a football, netball or cricket match at your local sports centre or sports ground.

For rather more money take a trip to the waxworks or a museum or art gallery, followed by a meal of burgers and chips.

TEN-TO-TWELVES

Don't even mention the word party to this age group. Parties are for little kids, in their estimation. On the other hand they still expect some kind of celebration on their birthdays. Dinner parties are all the rage for girls, with action-packed outings (to water centres, for example) favourite with boys. Adventure films (James Bond still reigns supreme) on the 'big screen' are acceptable; videos on the other hand are 'boring', mainly because they are often available at home. In some cases a disco works, but don't expect boys and girls to dance together as couples. Nowadays everyone bops along in a crowd.

Given that the world is their oyster, you might think the pre-teens could make up their minds. You'd be wrong. Members of this age group think they are adult. At times they even sound like adults, and some are tall enough to be; but deep down they're still kids. What they most want in the world is for the right thing to happen – by magic.

Consult them and they'll invariably mumble, hop from one foot to the other and eventually admit they don't know. Suggest something yourself and it will almost certainly be pronounced 'boring' (their favourite word). Be patient: after a week or so your own idea will probably be brought forward as a completely new and entirely original concept.

At least there's no problem about the food. Food for this group is good, old-fashioned, unhealthy junk-style take-away: hamburgers and chips or pizzas and milkshakes.

Once the entertainment has been chosen, all the perfect parent is expected to do is fund the exercise, supply the necessary transport and stay silent at all times. A parent's place is out of sight. On no account intrude on their non-conversations, or attempt to interrupt the vast acres of silence by making embarrassing remarks about your offspring's early childhood.

Your child is probably already deeply ashamed of you. Don't embarrass the other kids too.

CHAPTER 8

Other people's parties

Once you have given a few parties, you'll soon start to
develop a very clear idea of what makes a good guest. This
chapter gives you some points to bear in mind when the
tables are turned and you are on the receiving end of a
party. It also contains some information on a special type of
party at which you might be a guest – the charity ball.

HOW TO BE A GOOD GUEST
When you receive an invitation to a party, always answer
promptly. Arrive at the party on time, wearing the correct
clothes – if in doubt, ring up and check the form.

During the party, be genuinely more interested in others
than yourself and be prepared to please. Say nothing
unkind about anyone. Smile often and don't let yourself be
intimidated by crowds of strangers. In a room where you
know no one, approach a couple of friendly faces chatting
on the side of the room and ask if you may join them. Be
cheerfully honest: tell people you don't know anyone and
they are sure to help you.

Don't ever let your gaze wander away from the person to
whom you are speaking – it's both disconcerting and rude.
If someone does this to you at a party, smile sweetly, but
move away and leave him or her to forage for finer things
alone.

Read a newspaper, watch the TV news or listen to the
radio to keep abreast of current affairs. Being aware helps
keep general conversation going. In the bath before you
leave for the party, think of a few topics to talk about should
you find yourself seated next to a bore.

On no account drink too much, talk too loudly or get
uptight, and, when it's time to leave, simply stand up, shut
up, say goodbye, thank you and *go*.

If you're staying with friends it's a good idea to take along a present for the hostess. Chocolates or a plant are the obvious choice, but you might also consider giving one of the following – a box of luxury soaps, a new novel in hardback, pretty tea-towels, covered notebooks, a frilly cushion, or an eau de toilette spray of her favourite perfume. Don't forget to write a thank-you letter within a few days of leaving. Two to four lines saying you enjoyed yourself is quite sufficient.

CHARITY BALLS

If you want to dress up and dance the night away in a smart hotel, why not do it all in a good cause? Get your friends together and go to a charity ball.

Start planning in plenty of time and make up a good table. (Tables are usually for ten or twelve. Not many people go to a ball in a foursome.) Then send an early application together with your cheque to the chairman of the organizing committee.

Charity dances are not confined to any particular season, although organizers do tend to avoid August and September, when prospective ticket-buyers are presumed to be on holiday. January is unpopular too, for fear of empty pockets after Christmas. Otherwise choose your month or your favourite charity.

But before you dash off your cheque, do consider the consequences: one night at a charity ball is likely to set you back several hundred pounds. The tickets are at least £40 to £60 a head (and most self-respecting guests pay for their own), but that is only the beginning.

Here's a brief breakdown of likely expenditure to help you budget:

- dress: usually black tie for men and evening dress, long or short according to fashion, for ladies;
- drinks beforehand: you will have to meet up with your party somewhere; champagne at your home is the most economical solution; drinks in the bar at a club is the next best;
- transport: parking in city centres is often impossible; drinking and driving is another problem –

so unless one of you is teetotal by choice you'll probably need a taxi to and from the hotel;

- your meal is normally covered by the cost of the ticket; wines and other drinks, on the other hand, are not included; the hotel takes the profits from the drinks – not the charity;
- sundry expenses: these are not at all negligible when you add them up; from the minute you step inside the door, you and your guests are expected to smile and pay, pay, pay – for tombola tickets, raffle tickets, photos, programmes, silly balloons and, as if that were not enough, enter into the spirit of the auction;
- going 'on': there's always a chance some happy soul in your party will suggest slipping round to a nightclub. Join in and the cost goes on climbing; refuse and you'll be called a party pooper.

If you can afford this type of party, fine. If not, send your chosen charity a cheque, buy a bottle of wine, put the record-player on, and party at home.

It is undoubtedly flattering to be invited to join a charity ball committee, but my advice is to take care and think twice before you take up the offer. To be a useful committee member takes time and money. For a start you will certainly incur all the expenses listed above and in most instances quite a few more (committee members normally pay for their own tickets or at least their partner's); and the meetings are likely to take a terrible toll on your time and temper.

CHAPTER 9

Factfiles for planning parties

The following lists have been compiled to help you plan the perfect party. However, while the author has tried to ensure data is correct at the time of going to press, no responsibility can be accepted by author or publisher for the services offered.

Other useful sources of reference include society glossy magazines such as *Harpers and Queen* (especially the March issue), *Yellow Pages* and free local magazines.

PLACES FOR PARTIES
Any of the large hotels, for example, Dorchester, Claridge's, Savoy, Berkeley, Grosvenor House, Hilton, Inter-Continental, Inn on the Park, etc.

The Mall Galleries, 17 Carlton House Terrace, London SW1Y 5BD. Tel: 01-930 6844 (cocktail parties and weddings but no dancing)

The Orangery, Holland Park, c/o Town and Country Catering, Manor Farm Road, Alperton HA0 1BN

Hurlingham Club, Ranelagh Gardens, London SW6 3PR. Tel: 01-731 2909

Lord's Banqueting Centre, St John's Wood Road, London NW8 8QN. Tel: 01-286 1841

Four Seasons Restaurant, at the Inn on the Park, Hamilton Place, London W1A 1AZ. Tel: 01-499 0888 (accommodates 30)

Gay Hussar, 2 Greek Street, London W1V 6NB. Tel: 01-437 0973 (seats just 10)

Braganza Restaurant, 56 Frith Street, London W1V 5TA. Tel: 01-437 5412

Le Champenois, Cutlers Gardens Arcade, 10 Devonshire Square, London EC2M 4YA. Tel: 01-283 7888 (closed for the evening so can be hired for private parties)

The Roof Gardens, 99 Kensington High Street, London W8 5ED. Tel: 01-937 7994/8923

Tiddy Dol's Eating House, 55 Shepherd Market, London W1Y 7HL. Tel: 01-499 2357.

There are of course innumerable local wine bars or restaurants in other areas of London which are suitable for parties. The trouble is that many are here today and will be gone by the time this book is published. Field research, preferably on foot, is your best bet if you fancy a party in one of these areas.

Clubs (members only)
Annabel's, 44 Berkeley Square, London W1X 7RT. Tel: 01-629 3558
Institute of Directors, 116 Pall Mall, London SW1Y 5ED. Tel: 01-839 1233
United Oxford and Cambridge, 71 Pall Mall, London SW1Y 5HD. Tel: 01-930 5151
Boodles, 28 St James Street, London SW1A 1HJ. Tel: 01-930 7166 (Fridays only)
The Lansdowne Club, 9 Fitzmaurice Place, London W1X 6JD. Tel: 01-408 0246
Cavalry and Guards, 127 Piccadilly, London W1V 0PX. Tel: 01-499 1261
Many City livery halls (no dancing and they insist you finish quite early).

MARQUEE AND TENT CONTRACTORS
Black and Edgington Hire Ltd, 29 Queen Elizabeth Street, London SE1 2LU. Tel: 01-407 3734

Juliana's Party Organising Ltd, 1023 Garrett Lane, London SW17 0LN. Tel: 01-937 1555

C. F. Barker and Sons Marquees Ltd, 137 Dennett Road, Croydon CR9 2ST. Tel: 01-689 4191

Maidstone Marquee Hire Company Ltd, Milton Street, Maidstone, Kent ME16 8LL. Tel: 0622 691392

White Horse Marquees Ltd, Hill Deverill Manor, Warminster BA12 7SQ. Tel: 0985 40705

Modular Marquees, Flintham Cottage, Oaksey, near Malmesbury, Wilts SN16 9HS. Tel: 06667 246.

PARTY PLANNERS
This is a list of the most established organizations; you may find many others advertised elsewhere.

The Party Planners, Lady Elizabeth Anson, 56 Ladbroke Grove, London W11 2PB. Tel: 01-229 9666 (according to *Harpers and Queen* this company is 'quite the best to arrange everything most efficiently')

Joffins, 1 The Heliport Estate, Lombard Road, London SW11 3SS. Tel: 01-350 0033 (my own personal favourite)

Chatters, 10 Glenville Mews, London SW18 4NJ. Tel: 01-871 9455 (good, clear literature and helpful staff)

Chance Entertainment Ltd, 313 Brompton Road, London SW3 2DY. Tel: 01-584 3206 (claim to organize everyone and everything and their glossy brochure quotes an impressive list of satisfied clients)

Carol Hayes Associates, 191 Wardour Street, London W1V 3FA. Tel: 01-734 8883 (their exotic theme parties have been well publicized)

Bojolly's: see *Music Agents*.

Juliana's Party Organising Ltd: see *Marquees*.

FLORISTS
Pulbrook and Gould Ltd, 181 Sloane Street, London SW1X 9QW. Tel: 01-235 3920/3186

Constance Spry, 25 Manchester Square, London W1M 5AP. Tel: 01-486 6441

Moyses Stevens Ltd, 6 Bruton Street, London W1X 7AG. Tel: 01-493 8171

Felton and Sons Ltd, 220-224 Brompton Road, London SW3 2BD, tel: 01-589 4433, also at 6 Kimberley House, Holborn Viaduct, London EC1A 2AA, tel: 01-236 6308, and 5 Cheapside, London EC2V 6AA, tel: 01-236 7261

Edward Goodyear Ltd, 45 Brook Street, London W1Y 2JY, tel: 01-629 1508, also at 43 Knightsbridge, London W1Y 2JY, tel: 01-235 8344

Pugh and Carr Ltd, 26 Gloucester Road, London SW7 4RB. Tel: 01-584 7181

Molly Bloom's, 787 Fulham Road, London SW6 5HD. Tel: 01-731 1212

Petals Ltd, 112 Brook Drive, London SE11 4TQ

Ann Ord Flowers, 132 Bromwood Road, London SW11 6JZ.

FLOWER ARRANGERS
Flowers, Fiona Spring Rice, Fosseway House, Nettleton, Chippenham, Wilts SN14 7NL, tel: 0249 782875 and Sylvia Willis Fleming, Ducklings, Blackboys, Sussex TN22 5JA, tel: 082582 421 (between them they cover the UK)

Flowers and Co, Joanna Butterwick, Pickney's House, Pickney's Green, Maidenhead SL6 6QD and Tisha Monson, Keeper's Cottage, Hare Hatch, Reading, Berks. Tel: 073522 3960

Michael Goulding and Co, 79 St George's Square Mews, London SW1V 3RZ. Tel: 01-821 8621

Sonia Beresford Hobbs, Arch 57a, New Covent Garden Market, London SW8 5PP. Tel: 01-720 9345.

BALL GOWN HIRE
Cinderella (by appointment only), 29 St John's Avenue, London SW15 6AL. Tel: 01-789 8317

Dance Till Dawn, 23 Vicarage Gate, London W8 4BX. Tel: 01-937 2547

Hetherington, 289 Kings Road, London SW3 5EW

Paradi's, 41 Fairfax Road, London NW6 3RE. Tel: 01-372 6404

One Night Stand, 44 Pimlico Road, London SW1W 8LP. Tel: 01-730 8708

Hire charges usually range from about £60 upwards. Out of London you might find that a good dressmaker is a better option. If you live near an art school with a fashion design department, students are often only too happy to supplement their grant with a personal order.

ENTERTAINMENTS FOR CHILDREN'S PARTIES
John Hart (member of the Magic Circle), The Spinney, Shalden, Alton, Hants GU34 4DT. Tel: 0420 83239

Ronald Hayward, 14 St George's Road, Felixstowe, Suffolk IP11 9PL. Tel: 0394 272724

Smartie Artie (member of the Magic Circle), 57 Cutenhow Road, Luton, Beds LU1 3NB. Tel: 0582 459977

Kensington Carnival, 123 Ifield Road, London SW10 9AR. Tel: 01-370 4358/6384

Party Packs for Kids, 34 Devonshire Drive, London
SE10 8JZ. Tel: 01-692 3966

Fantastic Fireworks, PO Box 300, Redbourne, St Albans,
Herts AL3 7EE

Joe Manning and Son (for dodgems), Spurling Works,
Pindar Road, Hoddesdon, Herts. Tel: 0992 468862

Oscar's Den (for merry-go-rounds, trampolines, inflat-
ables, etc.), 15 Buckingham Palace Road, London SW1 0PP,
tel: 01-828 9300 and 127 Abbey Road, London NW6 4SL, tel:
01-328 6683.

MUSIC AGENTS
See your local *Yellow Pages* and the previously listed party
planners, almost all of whom act as agents for a multitude
of bands and discos.

Bojolly's, 421 Fulham Palace Road, London SW6 6SX. Tel:
01-371 0858

John Austin Organization, 25 Delamere Gardens, London
NW7 3EA. Tel: 01-959 1501

Joe Loss Agency Ltd, Morley House, Regent Street, London W1R 6QU. Tel: 01-580 1212/2323

Gordon Poole Agency, Kington House, Pierrepont Street,
Bath BA1 1LA. Tel: 0225 69884.

SECURITY
British Security Industry Association, PO Box 85, 46 Gill-
ingham Street, London SW1V 1HX. Tel: 01-630 5183. Make
sure the security firm you choose is a member of this
association.

Index

About the author

Helen O'Leary is a freelance home and cookery writer. She has written books on children's parties, cookery and home furnishings and is a regular contributor to women's magazines including *Cosmopolitan* and *Woman's Journal*. Her considerable party-giving experience ranges from large charity balls (such as the London Lifeboat Ball for 350 guests) to her own annual 'at home' event for 200 people, as well as numerous parties for her two children. She lives in Bristol.

Also from Columbus Books

COOKERY

Grub on a Grant Cas Clarke   Cheap and foolproof recipes for all student appetites   £3.95 net
One for All! Pam Dotter   Favourite dishes adapted for special diets   £5.95 net
Protein Power Margaret Leeming   Meatless meals in minutes   £3.95 net
Sinful Slimming Cas Clarke   How to lose weight by eating what you most enjoy   £3.95 net

SELF-HELP

How to Make It in the Rock Business Mary Wilson   £4.95 net
Taking Over Avril Rodway   How to cope with your elderly parents   £5.95 net
Help Yourself to Mental Health Mary Manning   How to beat stress and depression on your own terms   £4.95 net
Sex and the Single Parent Mary Mattis   How to combine an active social life with a good home life for your children   £4.95 net
I Love You, Let's Work It Out David Viscott M.D.   How to cope when a relationship runs off the rails   £5.95 net
Safe Sex Dr Elliot Philipp   The pleasures without the pitfalls   £1.95 net